On Common Ground

ON COMMON GROUND

De Prima Materia

Francis Reed

Working Press
London
1991

© Francis Reed 1991

British Library Cataloguing in Publication Data
Reed, Francis
On Common Ground
I Title
720

ISBN 1870736273

For a full list of titles please send a s.a.e. to
Working Press
85 St Agnes Place
London SE11 4BB

Typeset by GARD (Green Architectural Research and Design) Liverpool

Printed by Calvert's Press (TU) Workers' Co-operative
31/39 Redchurch Street · London E2 7DJ · Telephone 071-739 1474

Contents

"The Architect is one whose business is to do with everything"
R. Buckminster Fuller

"Woe unto them that lay house to house, that lay field to field till there be no place..."
Isiah 5.8.

Stone Stenness, Orkney.

Most of the drawings and photographs in this book were taken from life; part of the journey which gave it form.

Cover: front – Moorfields c.1559
back – Wall and window, Kings Lynn.

FOREWORD

The beginning is in the present, the places where we live - that other England, the rotting industrial cities of the North - and an attempt to understand the state of architecture, by looking at the relations which define its boundaries. Space is the basic material of architecture; 'Common Ground' expresses both the physical reality of the Common Lands - the great open spaces of the country, least touched by human intervention - and a kind of aboriginal dream or English 'Mythos'. In a sense it is 'the People', formed at once by the land and the collective unconscious. Carl Jung wrote that "primitive man dwells at once in his land and in the land of his unconscious" - an interplay of 'anima mundi' and 'genius loci' which prefigures architecture - and out of which it grows.The majority of Commons have been enclosed and dreams are manufactured in the mesmeric flicker of electrodes; but it is a wholeness that is buried, not lost.

Beyond a vague yearning for a 'quality of life', people are looking for an anchor (that is also a dream), in a world becoming ever more placeless and soulless. There is a need more than ever, for places which the psyche as well as the body can inhabit - "cars are parked, rats live, birds dwell; not many people dwell" as Ivan Illich puts it.

In a country over-enclosed, overcrowded and overloaded with industrial pollution, the Commons express something dwindling but crucial, a way of managing space together in harmony with the Earth. Architecture is about the way we treat each other; a social art defining space, inner and outer - with the capacity to act as a mirror, in which the analogous levels of landscape and memory become focussed on each other and the distinction seem transparent.

To move forward we need to be conscious of our origins - of our 'nature'; not in a way that undermines the present, but with a capacity for planetary vision, put into practice at a local scale. It may be as simple as a respect for the dust of which we are made, or the act of cutting a brick from the Earth, or an understanding, that "there is no wealth but life".[1]

1. John Ruskin.

BACKGROUND

The Commons tell a story of co-operation in human society and with the land (and of the gradual imposition of private interests), as fragments of the old 'cottage economy' in a present beset by totalitarian market forces and where the majority are outsiders in their own country.

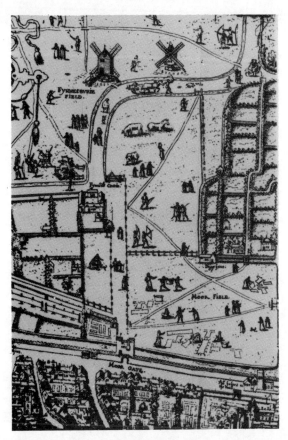

Moorfields Common c1559, from the earliest known map of London. On the reverse of the copper plate is a painting of the Tower of Babel; today much of the area is occupied by the hanging gardens of the Broadgate development.

"Let them not take in their commons, neither make parks nor pastures, for God gave the Earth for men to inhabit and not unto sheep and wild deer".

William Tyndale   1525

"Men fight and lose the battle and the thing they fought for comes about in spite of their defeat, and when it comes, turns out not to be what they meant, and other men have to fight for what they meant under another name".

William Morris   1888[1]

The Utopian dream has often been at its strongest during periods of national crisis and Socialist hope this century was forged in the experience of two World Wars. The Labour landslide of 1945 was brought about by a shared vision of a decent society for all, while the achievements of the Welfare State in turn brought complacency. It is the perreniel dilemma that confronts politicians of the Left, the danger that partial reforms anaesthetise people to themselves and to those around them.

Perhaps for Britain the last decade has been the step back after two steps forward : the machinery of a disappearing empire has been turned to self colonisation. London has been established as the World's financial capital, but at the expense of a lurch towards 'elective dictatorship'[2] to ensure investors' confidence. City institutions have feasted on the 'privatisation' of public assets with psychopathic zeal, less akin to 'selling off the family silver'[3] than Joyce's picture of Rome, living from the sale of ones mother's dead body. Even 'heritage' has become an industry.

The 'Free Market' was one of the ideological foundations of the Empire; today 'market forces' have distorted the life of the country - whether the disparity between regions or income groups - to the point where the Prime Minister could doubt the existence of society itself. Instead there is a limiting vision of "U.K. Limited"[4] where individuals are defined not by human relations but by their ability to consume. Those outside this crooked framework can simply be assumed not to exist; the unemployed condemned to anomie after at least thirty changes

6   in the method of computing statistics; the room not marked on the plans, 'where they turn blue'[5] in police stations built wth sound and video equipment to record events in every other; or the Poll Tax which has driven the poor off electoral registers into an amorphous mass of the governed[6] : a new serfdom.

The Commons form about 4.5% of the surface area of England and Wales (some 1.5 million acres out of 37 million); taken together, the 8,000 or so Commons would form an area the size of Linclonshire. Mainly the high ground of the country - 70% of the remaining English Commons are in the seven old Northern counties[7] and a further 16% are in the South West (Bodmin, Dartmoor, Exmoor, the Quantocks and Mendips) - they range from ancient forests like Ashdown, the New Forest and Epping, to the Dorset Heaths or Malvern Hills and mysterious mountains like Carn Ingli in the Preselis, where it is said Saint Brynach communed with angels and if anyone spends the night they will return either mad, or a poet. Oliver Rackham[8] makes a

Fylingdales Moor, January 1988 : 'holding a meeting on a subject of public interest' on Common Land in contravention of Military Bye-laws. W.G.Hoskins writes that the North Yorkshire Moors are "where Common Land plays its part in the life of the countryside to the maximum degree found anywhere at the present day".

distinction between heaths, moorland, fens and wood pasture (many 'forests' were predominantly heath - Sherwood was no more than 30% wooded at the Norman Conquest) and points out that Commons have a characteristic shape : "Commons, whether they be mere triangles of land where three roads meet or great tracts of heath or wood pasture, have an irregular concave outline, funnelling out into roads which cross the Common. This is the shape of a piece of land which it is no one person's duty to fence".[9] The 1958 Royal Commission on Common Land wrote of "the last reserve of uncommitted land in England and Wales" and was unable to locate more than a fraction of Welsh Common Lands. The Commons stand as a symbol of the immeasurable, in the face of "a civilisation which has chosen to turn its back on nature and quality in a desperate effort to measure and count everything";[10] and of the limits to central control.

The National Parks have been called the last jewel in the nation's crown; their heartland, "the remote and fortifying Commons",[11] stand aloof and untouched. Up here, what came to be called 'Thatcher's Britain' seems very small indeed; and a clearer view emerges - it is not 'Their' Britain but Ours.

"The Origins of Evil lie far back in time and it is one of the functions of history to trace them out".

G.M.Trevelyan

"A people without history is not redeemed from time, For history is a pattern of timeless moments... History is now and England".

T.S.Eliot[12]

"The origin of Common Land is a most obscure problem in English history... Common Rights were not something specifically granted by a generous landlord, but were the residue of rights that in all probability antedate the idea of private property in land, and are therefore of vast antiquity".[13] The Commons may be the remains of the earliest pastures, created by burning off scrub and woodland by people of the 'Middle Stone Age', roaming over the country with their newly domesticated herds of cattle[14]. As Bruce Chatwin puts it, there is "one characteristic of the Men of the Golden Age : they are always migratory... 'Nomos' is Greek for 'pasture' and the 'Nomad' is a chief or clan elder who presides over the allocation of pastures. Nomos thus came to mean 'law', 'fair distribution', 'that which is allotted by custom' and so the basis of all Western law".[15] If the Commons are 'the oldest institution in the land' - older than Crown, Parliament or Courts of Law - then it is because they are the land.

In their present form, Common Lands almost all belong to the Lord of the Manor, but local Commoners exercise rights of grazing (herbage), wood gathering (estovers), turf cutting (turbary), or fishing (pescary). The Manorial system is a legacy of the Norman Conquest, which although it destroyed the previous communality in land by force, was bound to acknowledge as rights what had always been the practice of the local population. These Rights of Common formed part of a broader system of co-operation within the Manor - arable land in common fields was divided into tenanted strips, both arable and pasture land were grazed by the tenants' stock after harvest and in fallow years, strict control was exercised over the numbers of stock allowed to graze both the pasture and Common Waste, and all these activities were organised by formal meetings of the Commoners.[16] At Laxton in Nottinghamshire, where due to a Nineteenth Century dispute between the Earls of Scarborough and Manvers a form of open field agriculture still operates, 'sykes' of grazing are kept between the arable strips and all villagers are entitled to bid when the syke grass is auctioned in July.

This contraposition of Commons and Lords, the democratic tendencies of what came to be seen as an Anglo-Saxon Golden Age and the Norman-French 'Yoke' is a key element in "the subtle network of compromises by which the nation keeps itself in familiar shape".[17] In allowing the continuation of the co-operative economy of the Commons, albeit dominated by the shadow of the castle and the horse - 'the sheepfold imposed on

the garden'[18] - the aristocracy ensured their own survival. Time
and again the English establishment has proved its resilience by
the ability to compromise and assimilate opposition.

Just as the village Green became the ground for archery and
the quintessentially English game of cricket, the greater
Commons have provided the back-drop to a continuous drama
in English history : "the enclosure of the land by the rich and
powerful and the encroachment on the land by the poor and
hungry".[19]

It was on Common land at Runneymeade that Magna Carta
was signed in 1215 and it was from Sherwood Forest (the 'Shire
Wood' Common to the County of Nottinghamshire) that Robin
Hood redistributed incomes, merging at once into the Wildwood
and into legend, as 'Jack in the Green' or the Green Man. The
Statute of Merton in 1235, however, extinguished certain rights of
access for the descendants of Commoners and extended the
power of the Barons. It was on Blackheath that Watt Tyler and
Jack Cade encamped after leading the Peasant Revolts of 1381
and 1449 to march on London. The 1381 Revolt was precipitated
by the introduction of a poll tax; John Ball preached that
"matters go not well to pass in England, nor shall they do, till
everything be common" and at its height, London was controlled
by an army of 100,000. Pacified and later betrayed by Richard II,
it nevertheless spelt the end of villeinage, as forced labour on
the Lord's estate was gradually replaced by the payment of rent.
These revolts were termed 'Risings of the Commons', referring as
much to the people as to the land; resistance to interference in
peoples' lives is often strongest where that connection lies
unbroken.

Enclosed, socially defined space and the untouched
wilderness form a polarity. We perceive through contrasts and
the Medieval landscape was full of such counterpoints, whether
the walled city and the fields without, or the sacred enclosure of
the churchyard and the village green. And in the balance
between the spiritual economy of the monastic cloister and the

peasant economy of individual strips in the open field and common grazing, Medieval society achieved something of an ideal relation between man and man and between man and the land. If the Earth was Christ's footstool, scripture and nature were the two sandals of Christ, according to Duns Scotus.[20]

"There is no particular merit in ancient things, but there is in integrity".[21] It is easy to romanticise the life of the Middle Ages; its ordered world view appeals in an age of uncertainty. Life was certainly lived in the shadow of war, famine, disease and, for the peasantry, ruthless exploitation - but the harshness and rigour of this common life, whether chanting the hours or working the land with the seasons, was also working with the grain of life in a way that brought about the spiritualisation of the commonplace. The Law of Sanctuary, that a man could take refuge from the secular authorities on consecrated ground - as at Durham and Beverley - for thirty-seven days and then flee the country, was equally a limit to the power of the Barons as were Common Rights. As a major landowner - holding as much as 30% of the country by the Reformation - the Church was a powerful check on Norman tyranny; and pilgrimage routes to shrines and holy places continued to follow ancient tracks and migration paths accross the landscape.

"Therefore that one covetous and unsatiable cormaurante and very plague of his native countrey maye compasse about and enclose many thousand of akers of grounde together within one pale or hedge, the husbandmen be thrust owte of their owne... "
Thomas More[22]

The Dissolution of the monasteries and the enclosure of the land are milestones in the creation of the present urban industrial system; and of an attitude that no longer sees matter as a vehicle for life, but as a resource from which energy can be extracted and used to control the rest of life. Sale of monastic property and hedged off fields produced the capital to finance a global trading empire abroad and the industrialisation of production at home. The main period of dissolutions was 1536-40 (the lesser houses having been dissolved in 1525). Acts

Byland Abbey

against enclosures passed in 1488 and 1514 were of little effect and already in 1549 foreign mercenaries had to be employed to crush a revolt against enclosures. In 1579, city financier Alderman Box submitted a scheme to Lord Chancellor Burghley for 'the division and ploughing up of the wastes of the country' although, as yet, it came to nothing.

Perhaps not all abbots were as concerned as Hugh of Avallon[23] who insisted that Henry II compensate the local peasantry for every penny of the value of land taken to establish a monastery at Witham in Somerset, but in the destruction of the monasteries much provision for the sick and poor was lost (parallel, perhaps, to what today is starved as a third rate 'voluntary sector').Dissolution and enclosures meant increasingly that the relation to the grain of life of the monks and cottagers was also dissolved and closed off, either as the preserve of a few, or subliminated and removed from reality. The Sixteenth Century sees the appearance of utopia ('no place') - at once a symptom of alienation and a sustaining vision in the face of it; an exodus from the land into the land of the imagination. More wrote his book in 1516, both from his own experience of monasticism and appalled at the enclosure of land for sheep runs - the same wool industry which brought the factory system - "your sheep that were want to be so meek and tame and so small eaters, now, as I heare saye, be become so great devourers and so wyld, that they eate up, and swallow downe the very men themselves".[24]

The memory of the monastic community became almost as recurrent an archetype in popular movements of the following centuries as cries of 'back to the land'. William Cobbett writes - "Mr Owen of Lanark, has it seems, been before the Committee with his schemes, which are nothing short of a species of monkery. This gentleman is for establishing innumerable communities of paupers! ...I do not understand whether the sisterhoods and brotherhoods are to form distinct communities like nuns and friars or whether they are to mix promiscuously"; or Benjamin Disraeli - "as for community, with the monasteries expired the only type we ever had in England".[25] It was also in the dissolution that squatting received royal sanction, when Henry VIII gave permission for the occupation of Black and Whitefriars in London.

"Therefore I say, the Common Land is my own land and equal with my fellow Commoners, and our true property by the law of creation. It is every ones, but not one single ones".

Gerrard Winstanley[26]

'Digger' and 'Leveller' were already terms in current usage during a Midlands revolt against enclosures in 1607 (and the sea-green banners of the Levellers were carried by West-Countrymen supporting the Duke of Monmouth at Sedgemoor in 1687), but it was during the 'English Revolution'that followed the Civil War of 1642-9 that they came into their own. At a point of precarious balance in this 'world turned upside down' the nation caught a momentary glimpse of itself before the fragments settled back into place. Many in the Parliamentary Army believed their victory had been a reconquest of the Land - that with the execution of the King, the Norman Yoke had been lifted - and 'who were the Barons but William the Conqueror's Colonels ?'.

While Sexby spoke for the Leveller faction at the Putney Debates - "There are many thousand of us soldiers that have ventured our lives; we have had little propriety in the Kingdom as to our estates, yet we have a birthright"[27] - some two hundred 'Diggers' led by William Everard and Gerrard Winstanley moved onto the Common at Saint George's Hill, Walton-on-Thames in April 1649 - "take notice that England is not a free people till the poor that have no land have a free allowance to dig and labour the Commons and so live as comfortably as the landlords in their enclosures".[28] The community built huts and grew beans, carrots and parsnips on the Common, but their presence as much as their ideas - "making the earth a common treasury for all, both rich and poor, that everyone that is born in the land may be fed by the earth his Mother that brought him forth"[29] - were not welcomed by neighbouring landlords.

Soldiers were sent to beat them in June; in the Autumn their crops and posessions were destroyed and the following March they were evicted and moved to Cobham Common, also in Surrey (today Saint George's Hill is a golf course and private housing estate where prices start at £600,000). Missionaries spread the movement to Common land in the counties of Kent, Hertford, Middlesex, Buckingham, Northampton, Leicester, Nottingham and Gloucester, but the main settlement at Cobham was evicted at Easter 1650 and an armed guard set on the Common, with threats of death issued if they returned. Many Levellers and Diggers were absorbed by the Quaker movement, inspired by George Fox after his vision on Pendle Hill (still Common Land) in Lancashire in 1652.

"The law locks up the man or woman.
Who steals the goose from off the Common,
But leaves the greater felon loose
Who steals the Common from the goose".

Anon.[30]

"But a bold peasantry, their country's pride,
When once destroyed, can never be supplied".

Oliver Goldsmith

In 1688 Gregory King estimated that there were 10 million acres of unenclosed 'waste' (the surface area of England and Wales is 37 million acres) where Common Land and open fields ran into each other; by 1850 over 6,600,000 acres of this had been enclosed by Act of Parliament.

Common Land Enclosures :

Years	Acts	Acres Enclosed
1750-1760	56	74,518
1761-1801	521	752,150
1802-1844	808	439,043
1845-	508	334,906
	1,893	2,100,617

Some 4.5 million acres of open field were also enclosed in 2,911 separate Acts during the same period.[31]

This tremendous acceleration of the rate and scale of enclosures exercised a profound effect on the country - in 1750 80% of the population lived in the country and 20% lived in towns; by 1830 the proportion had changed to 50% rural, 50% urban. Common Rights were the backbone of the 'Cottage Economy'[32] and had acted as a defence against starvation in lean years - from grazing and pollarding rights to peat, clay, gravel, coal or reed gathering. As it became possible to 'improve' Common Lands and convert them to profitable arable fields, land came increasingly to be seen as personal property and Common Rights as a feudal anachronism. Ironically, the abolition of feudal tenure in 1646 during the 'English Revolution ' had left the Commoner worse off, as landlords could now claim absolute ownership. As Professor Hoskins observes, as with the small farmer or shopkeeper today, so with the cottager, "somebody was after his property, with the noblest of motives and almost invariably in the national interest"[33] - a 'Wealth of Nations' founded on the poverty of the People and the 'robbery of the innocent unborn'. Hedges became the 'economic gravestone' of the peasantry, a new barrier between men and the land, artificially creating a whole new class, the labouring poor, whose "greatest offence against property was to have none".[34]

New gaols and Poor Law institutions sprang up, particularly after the 1834 Act which abolished all parish relief except the

Trinity Burial Ground, Hull - opened in 1794, the largest concentration of mature trees in the city centre and last remnant of Myton Carr, Hull's Common; within memory it was the only patch of land in the neighbourhood to graze a pony.

'Union' workhouse, often bordering remaining commons or occupying those enclosed. Prisons were built on Gloucester Green in Oxford, Myton Carr in Hull and along with a lunatic asylum on London's Wormwood scrubs; at Beverley Westwood a mental hospital and 'Poor Law Institution' were constructed. The remnants of the monastic pattern in the almshouses and charitable foundations disappeared with the coming of the Workhouse; embodying the abstract relationship between the State and a new proletariat.

The Commissioners of the Parliamentary Board of Agriculture savaged the Commons, much as Thomas Cromwell's Commissioners had dealt with the monasteries two and a half centuries earlier. Commons were found to be overgrazed or undrained; in reality there were elaborate local rules and customs to prevent over-exploitation. In Shropshire in 1794 they reported that Commoners' rights "afford them a very trifle towards their maintenance, yet operate on their minds as a sort of independence. The surrounding farmers by this means have neither industrious labourers or servants";[35] enclosure was presented as a public duty in the interests of social discipline. The East Riding of Yorkshire, was second only to the East Midlands in the severity of enclosures; at Hornsea, on the coast North East of Hull, Whitsun week was a succession of dinners and dances culminating in a coronation of the 'Ladies of the Pasture' - with enclosure all this disappeared.[36]

It was a great irony that the Acts of Enclosure were passed by a 'House of Commons' from which the majority were disenfranchised. It was taken as an omen when Parliament burnt down on the night of 16th October 1834.

Many of the expropriated faced starvation, while for landowners enclosure usually meant higher yields, higher prices and higher rents. Corn Laws were passed to protect the interests of the rich, in the face of bad harvests and blockades, as the Napoleonic Wars became the forcing house for the Industrial Revolution. "The beautiful and romantic valleys of Derbyshire, Nottinghamshire and Lancashire secluded from the public eye,

became the solitudes of torture, and many of murder".[37] Children
were stolen to work the mills from workhouses in London and
Birmingham and outside Oldham, the Common Moor
disappeared under eight cotton mills and two hundred and thirty

Liverpool, port for the slave trade and the Lancashire cotton industry is
the largest of several towns and cities to stand on Common Land, in this
case belonging to the parish of West Derby.

six houses; 'employment' became as much an expropriation of
time as the enclosures were of space.

It was found that steam would power machinery in the woolen
mills as well as water, and from this grew the marriage of coal
and iron which forged the industrial domination of the world; at
once an unconscious process and one unopposed and
unquestioned by those who stood to gain. As Doctor Johnson
put it : "I know that the world is a confused place... and that I
benefit from this confusion".

"The commercial expansion, the enclosure movement, the early years of the Industrial Revolution - all took place within the shadow of the gallows".[38]

Tearing down fences around newly enclosed Common Land was a capital offence, but many enclosures were repulsed and many other Commons defended to the last. William Cobbett succesfully championed the cause of Horton Heath in East Dorset : "The cottagers produced from their little bits, in food for themselves, and in things to be sold at market, more than any neighbouring farm of two hundred acres. I came to hate a system that could lead English Gentlemen to disregard matters like these. That could induce them to tear up 'wastes' and sweep away occupiers like those I have described. Wastes indeed; give a dog an ill name. Was Horton Heath a waste ? Was it a 'waste' when a hundred, perhaps, of healthy boys and girls were playing there of a Sunday, instead of creeping about covered in filth in the alleys of a town ?".[39] Today Horton Heath remains and is a Site of Special Scientific Interest; "Heathland is an ancient and beautiful part of our heritage. It is a symbol of liberty... the voices of Gilbert White, John Clare, George Borrow and Thomas Hardy reminded us of the glory and mystery and freedom of the heath. But few listened : heathland is something that people do not value until they have lost nine-tenths of it."[40]

Professor Hoskins relates the story of the protracted struggle for the 4,000 acres of Otmoor in Oxfordshire, where the cottagers made £1 annual profit from cattle grazing. In 1801 the Duke of Marlborough petitioned Parliament unsuccessfully for its enclosure, but in 1809 the Board of Agriculture filed an unfavourable report and in 1815 an Enclosure Act received the Royal Assent. The cottagers were bought out by speculators, but direct action continued. In 1829 twenty two farmers were aquitted on felony charges for cutting new embankments and on September 6th five hundred commoners and five hundred supporters marched the seven mile boundary removing fences. The Riot Act was read and forty four arrests made, but the charges of unlawful assembly received sentences of no longer than four months, due to the strength of public feeling. Cattle grazed the Common once again and a Defence Association was established. Fences were torn down again at every full moon, with Otmoor remaining in a state of rebellion throughout the 1830's; and "all the destruction, ill feeling and expense produced only unimproved pasture instead of the arable land which Arthur Young had predicted"[41] in 1809. "In the mid-Twentieth Century, Otmoor is used as a bombing range, a marked advance over the simple common grazing of the Dark Ages".[42]

For many in the industrial towns, access to the land had now become a utopia and they flocked to join Fergus O'Connor's 'Chartist Land Company'. Established in 1845 to return people to enough land to make them eligible to vote, it soon had 70,000 subscribers in 60 branches and a £90,000 share issue. By 1847 there were 600 farmers chosen by ballot, in settlements with names like 'Charterville' and 'O'Connorville'; although the villages remain, the company was wound up and the estates sold in 1851 after a Parliamentary Enquiry into its activities.

The Enclosure Act of 1845 made provision for land to be set aside for purposes of exercise and recreation and for the poor in compensation for the loss of Common Rights. In practice this was obstructed by the landowners; the 1834 Poor Law Commission had reported that "We can do little or nothing to prevent pauperism; the farmers will have it : they prefer the labourers to be slaves".[43]

The 1842 Select Committee on the Labouring Poor (Allotments of Land) recommended that allotments to the labourer "should not become an inducement to neglect his usual paid labour".[44] Rented at anything between 40% and 500% more than adjoining land, they came to be seen as an act of charity rather than the fragmentary vestige of ancient rights. Often it was only the support of sympathetic clergy which ensured their provision - the farmers being ever wary that the process of taking with one hand might give too much back with the other (in Twentieth Century America, Henry Ford promoted allotments, believing they would keep his workers' minds off politics but not away from the production line, while Frank Lloyd Wright was considered a Left-Wing extremist for his self-sufficient vision of 'Broadacre City'). Of 320,000 acres of Common Land enclosed between 1845 and 1869 only 2,000 acres were allotted for labourers and cottagers.

Railway Allotments, Hull : the area supports a good ecology of wild birds and butterflies, apple trees,sheep, horses, a meadow of goats, pigeon lofts and poultry as well as allotments growing flowers, fruit and vegetables.

The rate of enclosures slowed considerably in the 1870's; in 1873-4 a census was held of the remaining 2.5 million acres of Common and after the 1876 Commons Act, future enclosures were carefully scrutinised by a Select Committee. In 1884 Gladstone gave the vote to agricultural labourers and the 1887 Allotments Act made the provision of allotments an obligation of Councils in rural districts (only extended to urban local authorities in 1907). "Why should we be beggars with the ballot in our hand - God gave the land to the people !" as the Land Song[45] put it; while Wiliam Morris' "News from Nowhere"(1890) inspired the beginnings of Socialism with a vision of England as "a garden where nothing is spoilt and nothing is wasted". The end of the century saw the emergence of the familiar urban landscape of the housing estate - "barracks in truth, housing for the army of industrialism"[46] - and the allotment.

In 1913 there were between 400,000 and 600,000 allotments; the number swelled to over a million at the end of the two world wars - in the First War 2 million tons of vegetables were produced annually, while in the Second War, 10% of all food and a quarter of all eggs came from allotments.[47] Today, when many more people have gardens, there are still more than half a million allotments and gardening remains our most popular leisure pursuit. Yet financial pressure on bodies as diverse as the Church, the Railways and Local Authorities to 'realise' their assets has brought allotments under increasing threat. Durham Cathedral has abandoned its plan to sell Saint Margaret Street allotments only after a vociferous two and a half year campaign in the city[48] - "this is Durham's Mappa Mundi" as one tenant put it. In Hull, British Rail have cut off the water supply to allotments worked continuously by the same men for over sixty years 'due to operational requirements', while the City Council is selling 40 of its 190 acres and planning to compulsorily purchase allotment land at Reed's Lane in the hope of making £750,000 profit by its resale for housebuilding.

If Wartime saw the number of allotments at its height, it also saw the appropriation of Common Land for use as battle training areas or airfields and between 80,000 and 90,000 acres are still occupied by the military. The Defence Act of 1854 allowed the War Office to use procedures in the 1845 Enclosure Act to extinguish Common Rights; at least seventeen Surrey Commons near Aldershot have been occupied by the Army since the 1860's (and other Commons in this area 'have tended to disappear') and much of Dartmoor has been in use as military ranges since 1875.

15,000 acres of Common belonging to four moorland parishes at Fylingdales in North Yorkshire were requisitioned for training

Saxon Cross on Lilla Howe, Fylingdales Moor - the 'Phased Array Radar' pyramid can be seen under construction in the distance.

purposes during the Second World War, but never returned as promised. The present Early Warning and Satellite Intelligence Station was built by the U.S. Air Force in 1961-2 and in 1963 L.Dudley Stamp wrote that "their continued use is scarcely compatible with the designation of the whole area as a National Park".[8] It probably played a role in the guidance of so-called 'smart' weapons in the Gulf War, while the pyramid shaped 'Phased Array Radar' system currently under construction forms part of the 'Star Wars' strategy.

Of 2,000 acres of Common at Lakenheath in Suffolk, one half is a Site of Special Scientific Interest and the other is a U.S. Air Force base, from which nuclear capable F111 bombers took off to attack Libya in May 1986. Hardened concrete hangars for nuclear 'Tactical Air to Surface Missiles' are now under construction and there is the possibility - fifty years after the Battle of Britain - of the Luftwaffe having a base there.

634 out of 856 acres of Greenham Common in Berkshire were requisitioned together with 407 acres of neighbouring Crookham Common to build an airfield during the Second World War;[50] once noted for its butterflies, Greenham came to prominence as the base for American 'Cruise' missiles in 1983, for the Womens' Peace Camp and as a focus for protest in the Peace Movement that became one of the great popular political forces of the century. It has also been the subject of a series of interesting legal cases concerning Common Rights. In February 1988 Military Byelaws were ruled out of order at Reading Crown Court and although this judgement was overturned by the High Court in October 1988, it transpired that Commoners still have the right to quarry gravel under the runway; an appeal was lodged with the House of Lords, who ruled in June 1990 that the byelaws were indeed illegal. Women entering the base can no longer be detained or charged, while those already convicted of trespass are claiming compensation.

In March 1988 the legitimacy of the base was challenged under the 1925 Law of Property Act and the case continues, since which time the Ministry of Defence has sought to buy the Commoners Rights or extinguish them under the 1854 Defence

Greenham Common, September 1988 : the hardened concrete silos
contained 96 nuclear 'cruise' missiles, more than thirteen hundred times
the explosive force of the bomb that wiped out Hiroshima in 1945.
Property Services Agency architects received a 'design award' from the
United States Air Force for the water tower on the horizon.

Act; in May 1991 an alleged £80,000 compensatuion was paid
into an account after four of the thirty four refused to co-operate.
However, the County Court ruled in August 1988 that the 1854
Act does not provide for compulsory purchase or extinction
(extinction of Common Rights by the War Office at Strensall near
York required a separate Act of Parliament). The Act was
intended only to provide for the defence of the realm, while it is
probable that the Ministry is motivated by the commercial
potential of the land; it is now possible that the Commoners will
make a challenge in the courts or appeal for a judicial review of
attempts at deregistration.

Regular tearing down of the perimeter fence is reminiscent of
the resistance to Enclosure or the Luddites and Machine Breakers
of the early Nineteenth Century, while on the other side of the
fence the Security Service (MI5) continues to operate under the
claim of Crown Prerogative outside Parliament. The missiles have
been flown back to America under the 'Intermediate Nuclear
Forces' treaty with the Soviet Union, but it is inconceivable that
the agreement would have been signed if 'Cruise' had not
become a political embarrassment. Now a group headed by local
worthies Richard Adams and Lord Denning, calling itself

'Commons Again' is campaigning for the return of the land to its
former state.

"History has remembered the kings and the warriors, because they destroyed; Art has remembered the people because they created" as William Morris wrote; the contrast of swords and ploughshares is stark. Technological development seems always to have led to the subjection of the majority - and the use of land as a source of income for the military. The Dane-Geld, one of the earliest taxes in England, was levied to support the occupying Danish army; Norman feudalism firmly established the principle, with land held in return for military service. The poll tax which sparked the Peasants' Revolt of 1381 was intended to finance the Hundred Years' War with France.

The outbreak of both World Wars thwarted long campaigns by the urban majority to re-establish a stake in the land - the 1913 Land Tax and the 1939 Access to Mountains Bill were both set aside in the interests of 'national unity' - yet in the aftermath of war people felt they had a right to the land they had fought for, irrespective of legislation. In 1945 returning soldiers occupied empty camps and mansions, with a renewed understanding that "the power of enclosing land and owning property was brought into creation by your ancestors by the power of the sword".[51] As the fourth largest arms exporter in the World, military technology now forms the backbone of Britain's industry, yet we lack any real agricultural base, with the people of the 'Third World' now cast in the role of peasantry.

If the Commons are seen as 'relics of low intensity agriculture', "another thirty years of huge economic incentives for the maximisation of food production, coupled with the exclusion of farming operations from our planning machinery will mean the end of the English landscape as we know it".[52] Quiet and insidious changes in the scale of farming have impoverished the face of the country, as rough, marginal places - meadows, marshes, ditches or woods - which give the landscape character and interest are ploughed away. Hedges are being torn up at a rate of 4,000 miles a year - 'market forces' mean 'prairie farming' and fields that stretch further than the eye can see. The Ministry of Agriculture aimed to have all chalk downland - even the steep valley sides - in Humberside 'improved' by 1990. In practice this means biologically impoverished fields of rye grass - the new Wastes.

The establishment of agricultural subsidies and price linked production goes back to the Corn Laws which fixed prices during the Napoleonic Wars (in force 1815-1846), yet recent concern about salmonella in eggs, listeria in dairy produce or B.S.I. in beef serve to highlight the problems of modelling biological processes on the factory system. The E.C. 'Common Agricultural Policy' is estimated to cost each household £1,000 per year and while it has been announced that this is to be cut by 30%, there is talk of taking as much as 10 million acres 'out of agricultural production'. It is argued that Britain has been unable to feed itself without imports since the population rose above 20 million in the Nineteenth Century (Kropotkin, however, boldly claimed that intensive horticulture could feed 90 million[53]), but this is no reason for diminishing our capacity any further. Where the average size of farm in 1906 was 63 acres, today it is nearer 270 acres[54] and while family farms are still numerous, they only occupy a fraction of the land. Over 300 small 'Land Settlement Association' farms (tenanted from the Ministry of Agriculture) operated profitably in ten locations until 1982, when they were wound up due to innefficient management in Whitehall, who were responsable for marketting the produce - the tenants are collectively suing the Ministry for £2.7 million. Lincolnshire, Cambridgeshire, and Norfolk County Councils still rent a large number of smallholdings, yet in the 1930's Wal Hannington warned that "those who advocate land settlement under capitalism as a solution for industrial unemployment are either blind to the consequences of such a policy or they are deliberately deceiving the unemployed".[55]

The landscape is also coming under increasing threat from building development - Lawrie Barratt, the first man to treat the house as a consumer durable, has been allowed to hold a lobby for the 'release' of green belt land for speculative housing at 10 Downing Street. The utopian image of the country cottage, whose independent existence was extinguished when the Commons were enclosed, conceals a mortgage system and rising house prices which operate as a powerful form of social control. It also creates a kind of apartheid between home owners and those in local authority housing, or between comfortable suburbs and older centres, which become reservations of the urban poor. "Wherever I drive in Southern England today, the place is being torn up and torn apart",[56] writes Micheal Heseltine, who as Defence Minister supervised the eviction of women campers at Greenham and the settlers at Molesworth in February 1985. But perhaps the ultimate wilderness of The Bomb and the flimsy enclosure of the Barratt House are part of the same phenomenon; of a mentality that catalogues land on library shelves at 333 next to property and is prepared to destroy it in order to defend it. It was the same Harold Macmillan who coined the term 'property owning democracy' who suggested that "the British people are prepared... to be blown to atomic dust". House building as a social activity was part of the cottage economy; since its demise 'housing' has been used as a palliative for the ills of urban deprivation - as George V put it in 1919 : "if 'unrest' is to be converted into contentment, the provision of good houses may prove one of the most potent agents in that conversion"[57] and the Hull Garden Village was built by Sir James Reckitt in 1911 to prevent a "disastrous uprising". If economic "growth is nothing more than the ever more perfect technical reproduction of what you were already doing, prevented by law, and sold back as fashion",[58] this is nowhere clearer than in the field of housing. The government gives £7 billion annually in mortgage tax relief, but home ownership can never be a blanket solution to Marx' three-fold alienation, from self, from others and from nature.

The 1925 Law of Property Act established public access to all Commons lying within Metropolitan Districts - pressure from landed interests forced the withdrawal of proposals for access to

Common Land in all parts of the Country. A 1947 Committee on Footpaths and Access recommended a universal right of access to "enable active people of all ages... to discover for themselves the wild and lonely places, and the solace and inspiration they can give to men who have been 'long in city pent'" - but the 1949 National Parks and Access to the Countryside Act provided only for access agreements to be negotiated site by site. The 1986 Common Land Forum of the Countryside Commission reported that legal right of access is thus restricted to only one fifth of the 1.5 million acres remaining in England and Wales, and once again recommended that this be extended to all Commons. The same recommendations were made by the 1955-58 Royal Commission but in the 1986 report 'universal right of public access' was whittled down to 'persons on foot for purposes of quiet enjoyment',[59] and in spite of Conservative

Newcastle Town Moor, most famous and extensive of the urban Commons, said either to have been given to the townsmen by Adam de Jesmond in the Thirteenth Century,or held by the Burgesses from the Crown since time immemorial. Today there are allotments, a race course and a gypsy encampment, as well as Common grazing.

election promises in 1987, the prospect of legislation seems no nearer - the country landowners' lobby remains as powerful an influence as ever.[60] Specious arguments are put forward about 'wildlife conservation' on upland grouse moors, while the National Farmers' Union has pleaded that "Common Land is in fact private land and... Rights of Common enjoyed on it may be vital to the viability of many farms".[61] According to the Swedish Ambassador, "the right of public access, known in Sweden as Allemansrat (the right of all men), is a right which goes back to time immemorial... It must be remembered that the right of access also entails obligations - members of the public... must show due consideration to landowners as well as to other people and to flora and fauna".[62] In Scotland the Law of Trespass states that everyone has a right of passage, although only the owner has a right of use; what is enjoyed in Sweden as a right and in Scotland at the landowner's discretion, is enjoyed in England hardly at all.

From being an expression of communal ownership and relation to the land, Commons were first reduced to surface working rights and now to purposes of recreation. Perhaps this parallels the removal of the bulk of industrial production to developing countries, that has made leisure as much as labour an exploitable resource - as the relation between management and workers is replaced by one between management and 'the Community', people and bureaucracy. Privatisation and asset stripping of British concerns has put workers on the dole rather as enclosures sent cottagers to the workhouse; and may not the new generation of 'Theme Parks' be successors of the Works Estate and the Baronial Enclosure ? Or indeed Lord Marshall's thwarted intention to turn the country into a nuclear 'science park' (at Harwell, redundant reactors are soon to become a museum because of the risks of de-commissioning).

The 1957 Winfrith Heath Act abolished Common Rights on all but 77 acres out of 793 acres in Dorset to make way for the U.K. Atomic Energy Authority's experimental reactors (today there is an above average rate of leukaemia among local children) and the Magnox reactor at Trawsfynydd stands on Common Land in North Wales purchased by the War Office in 1905. The latest proposal, for a third reactor at Hinckley Point in Somerset, has been shelved, but objectors at the Public Enquiry faced the same prohibitive legal costs as those who petitioned Parliament against enclosures at the beginning of the Nineteenth Century. Lewis Mumford contrasted the Mega-machine at Trawsfynydd with the charm of neighbouring Portmerion, the holiday village built from scratch;[63] but may they not be two sides of the same coin - a nostalgia for the past and an adulation of the future which both avoid the present ?[64]

A Return of Ownership in 1874, intended to show that land was no longer the preserve of a few, in fact confirmed the opposite - the first survey of its kind since William the Conqueror compiled Domesday Book in 1086, showed 75% of the land in Britain was owned by 7,000 families, with 25% of this owned by 710 individuals. Today 1% of the population still own 75% of the land and 30% is owned by 1,700 individuals - of whom 300 are peers and 700 members of old families of the landed gentry.[65] The 400 richest individuals in the country own 4.4 million acres between them and 103 of them are members of the aristocracy.[66] The general pattern of large scale land tenure has changed little in the last few centuries; what have been sacrificed are the small proprietor and the Common Rights of the majority, in the cause of Empire and enormous gains for the few. In the process, much of the indigenous culture of England was destroyed, leaving the aristocracy with an apparent monopoly on the nation's heritage. From the sturdy independence of the cottage, the Englishman's house became his castle; and when, in the 1920's and 30's, increased leisure allowed working people to build weekend houses in Essex or along the Yorkshire Coast, these shanties were 'little country houses' rather than 'little houses in the country'. There is, albeit unconsciously perhaps, a tragic aspiration for the wealth, power and privacy of the landed elite in the carriage lamps and Brazilian mahogany fan-light doors of 'cottage-style starter homes'. What Orwell described as the 'restless, cultureless life' of light industry and arterial roads, has become the fantasy world of Theme Parks, 'Heritage Experiences', gambling arcades and video tape, used to block the pain of separation from the intimate connection between land and culture. Before being packaged and sold, there is a kind of butchery of memory; the waxworks at Madame Tussaud's, our most popular tourist attraction, have their origin in the death masks of the Paris Terror, while 'The Tales of Robin Hood' at Nottingham uses abattoir technology to transport visitors through the series of tableaux - people themselves are treated as dummies without capacity for imagination.

Only 1.38% of land in National Parks is actually publicly owned[67] and in spite of owing their existence to large areas of Common, the Parks have tended to manage the visual appearance of the landscape in the national interest, often at the expense of local culture and livelihoods. While the Atlee Government's failure to nationalise the land in 1945 was in some ways lamentable (future land reform might be better directed at redistribution, with checks to prevent reconcentration), the 1.6 million membership and land holdings of 200,000 acres make the National Trust our largest voluntary organisation (with its origins in the Commons Defence Association of the last Century). Yet perhaps it has become more a part of the nostalgia cult of 'Heritage' and the Country House, than a means for people to regain a stake in the land. Established in 1895 with the intention of "accepting, holding and purchasing open spaces for the people in town and city", "the trust has evolved into a major safety net for preventing the decline and fall of the English stately home... from being an egalitarian access organisation promoting the public good, the trust has become an elitist club"[68] and has even been enclosing Common Land on the Gower Peninsular in South Wales.

The green road verges of a parish originally formed part of the Common, but villagers had to pay to graze animals on the new enclosure roads; today motorways consume 40 acres of land per mile and with 24 million cars in Britain there is one for every 15 metres of road. Motor transport has brought the freedom of mobility, but at enormous cost in resources and to the environment. Richard Maybey points out that when city dwellers visit the country, they are in a sense coming home;[69] an estimated 16 million people visit the country on an average Summer Sunday. Britain in the 1990's is a predominantly urban society - where half the population worked the land in 1750, today 80% of the land surface is worked by 2.5% of the population - but new areas of wilderness have appeared in our towns, whether the result of bombing, slum clearance or industrial decline.

Australian Aboriginal film maker Rikki Shields says he finds Britan the most imprisoned country he has visited in Europe, because our land and sacred sites have been enclosed (apposite coming from one whose country was used as a British penal colony; in fact one in every thousand Britons is in custody and only Turkey and Austria have a larger proportion of their

City Farm, Rotherhithe; sheep grazing in the shadow of Canary Wharf - a monument to the Thatcher years, built with an estimated £900 million of public subsidy.

population behind bars[70]). "They give people a little piece of green, a park, otherwise they would kill the master".[71] In 1989 one in every hundred 17-21 year olds was in prison; we spend £1 billion annually on the prison service and £1 billion new investment is under way. The Maximum Security Wing at Full Sutton near York cost £20 million to house twelve prisoners; plaster is changed every three months to replace bugs and sensors.

For many the Poll Tax has ammounted to little more than a return to the days of paying the gaoler : a disabling tax on existence, where the least advantaged pay to be kept poor, imprisoned in a total cash economy.[72] A local policeman talks of suicides in Hull's high rise blocks of flats : "a bit of green, that's what stops them going over the top".[73] Our understanding of the Commons needs to be a sustaining vision in the face of self colonisation, rather than a rustic illusion; helping us to work from these green spaces to transform cities from the inside, with a sense of the landscape - real and psychological - that underlies our urban areas.

NOTES

1. 'A Dream of John Ball' 1888
2. Lord Hailsham, Conservative Lord Chancellor.
3. Harold Macmillan, Lord Stockton.
4. John Duke, Chief Constable of Hampshire, evicting Stonehenge Festival goers at Stoney Cross, New Forest 10.6.86.
5. Anecdotal, August 1988, from architect working for the Property Services Agency.
6. Significantly, the 'Community Charge' Bill was only passed in the House of Lords (23.5.88.) by securing an attendance of 500, unequalled this Century except by the 1971 vote on E.E.C. membership.
7. Northumberland, Westmorland, Cumberland, Durham, Lancashire, Yorkshire and Derbyshire.
8. Oliver Rackham : 'The History of the Countryside' Dent 1986.
9. Ibid.
10. Keith Critchlow : 'Return from Exile' in 'The Land' Gordon Fraser 1975
11. Royal Commission on Common Lands 1958. It was the large proportion of Common remaining in these areas which enabled the establishment of the National Parks in 1947 - for instance 30% of Breconshire, 25% of Westmorland and 16% of North Yorkshire were Common.
12. 'Little Gidding', 'Four Quartets' 1944.
13. W.G.Hoskins in Hoskins and L.Dudley Stamp : 'The Common Lands of England and Wales' Collins 1963.
14. Christopher Taylor : 'Roads and Tracks of Britain' Dent 1979.
15. Bruce Chatwin : 'The Songlines' Pan 1988
16. Christopher Taylor : 'Fields in the English Landscape' Dent 1975.
17. George Orwell : 'The Lion and the Unicorn - Socialism and the English Genius' 1941.
18. Chatwin op.cit.

19. Colin Ward in Colin Ward and David Crouch : 'The Allotment' 1988.

20. John Duns the Scot (c1265-1308) taught in Oxford , where his detractors lent his name to the expression 'dunce'.

21. Edward Hyams : 'Soil and Civilisation' Thames and Hudson 1952.

22. Thomas More's 'Libellus Vere Aureus Nec Minus Salutaris quam Festivus de Optima Reip. Statu deque Nova Insula Utopia' was first published in Louvain in 1516, but the first English edition did not appear until Ralph Robinson's translation : 'Utopia or the best state of a Republic Weal' of 1551.

23. Later Saint Hugh of Lincoln (1135-1200).

24. Thomas More op.cit.

25. Benjamin Disraeli : 'Sybil or the Two Nations' 1845.

26. Gerrard Winstanley : 'New Year's Gift for Parliament and Army' 1652 in Colin Ward : 'The Early Squatters' in 'Squatting : the Real Story' ed. Nick Wates 1980.

27. In A.L.Morton : 'The English Utopia' Lawrence and Wishart 1978.

28. In Ian Tod and Micheal Wheeler :'Utopia' Orbis 1978.

29. Winstanley : 'The True Levellers' Standard Advanced' in 'The Law of Freedom and Other Writings' ed. Christopher Hill Penguin.

30. A similar Epigram appeared in 'The Tickler' magazine in 1821

31. Hoskins op.cit.

32. This was the title of a book by William Cobbett published in 1821; a kind of self-sufficiency manual in which advice on brewing, breadmaking, and the keeping of geese, poultry, pigs and cows are interspersed with tirades against tea, potatoes and factory made clothes.

33. Hoskins op.cit.

34. E.P. Thompson : 'The Making of The English Working Class' Gollancz 1963.

35. In Hoskins op.cit.

36. Jan Crowther : 'Enclosure Commissioners and Surveyors of the East Riding' East Yorks. Local History Society 1986.

37. Sir F.M.Eden quoted in Karl Marx : 'Capital' 1885.

38. E.P.Thompson op.cit.

39. 1830 quoted in Richard Maybey : 'The Common Ground' Nature Conservancy Council and Hutchinson 1980

40. Rackham op. cit. Poole and Bournemouth continue to expand onto surrounding heathland, including 'Sites of Special Scientific Interest'; Poole is entirely sited on Common Heathland.

41. Ibid.

42. Hoskins op.cit.

43. in Crouch and Ward op. cit.

44. Ibid.

45. in Marion Shoard : 'This Land is Our Land' Paladin 1988.

46. George Gissing in Lionel Esher : 'A Broken Wave : The Rebuilding of England 1940-1980' Lane 1981.

47. Crouch and Ward op. cit.

48. L.D.Stamp op. cit.

49. Guardian 9.7.90.

50. R.A.F. evidence to Royal Commission on Common Land 1958.

51. Gerrrard Winstanley : "A declaration from the poor oppressed people of England directed to all that call themselves or are called Lords of the Manors" 1649.

52. Marion Shoard : 'The Theft of the Countryside' Temple Smith 1980

54. Richard Norton-Taylor : 'Whose Land is it Anyway?' Turnstone 1982.

55. In 'Land for the People' ed. Herbert Girardet Crescent 1976.

56. Guardian 14.3.87.

57. In John Burnett : 'A Social History of Housing 1815-1970' 1978.

58. 'Art in Ruins' Glyn Banks and Hannah Vowles Essay Liverpool 1991.

59. Countryside Commission : Common Land Forum Report 1986.

60. The Labour Party has promised to implement the Common Land Forum Report if elected (August 1990) and create new National Parks in England, probably in the New Forest and the South Downs.

61. Norton-Taylor op. cit.

62. Lief Liefland in 'Head for the Hills - The Right to Roam' : Ramblers' Association pamphlet 1990.

63. In the epilogue to Clough Williams-Ellis : 'England and the Octupus' 1975 edition Portmerion (first published 1928).

64. Basil Spence was equally able to design Coventry Cathedral as this temple to nuclear technology. There is an apocryphal story that he took the idea for the zig-zag wall plan of the cathedral from a sliding door to the Nuclear Engineering building at Glasgow University.

65. Norton-Taylor op. cit. The Thatcher Government announced an end to the collection of statistics relating to income and wealth in 1981.

66. Sunday Times 16. 9.90.

67. Marion Shoard : 'This Land is Our Land'.

68. Rodney Legg of the Open Spaces Society, interviewed in The Guardian 23.10.90.

70. Guardian 18.4.87.

71. Visit to Hull 19.6.88.

72. Northampton, whose County was perhaps the most severely enclosed - leaving only forty Commons, few more than an acre - was the first to employ bailiffs against Poll Tax defaulters; and the first non-payer to be imprisoned (7.12.90.) was 20 year old Brian Wright from Mrs Thatcher's native Grantham.

73. P.C. Green October 1988.

COMMON GROUND

In the 'Gothic' architecture of the Middle Ages there is a paraphrase of the forms of nature because of the way in which the men who built it were working; they did not have our dualism of spirit and matter - seeing a gradation of mixtures of the two- any more than our separation of hand and brain in practice. The 'winter' of the 'Rennaissance' brought this cycle to an end - as the making of architecture became increasingly constrained.

The European domination of the world in the colonial era was a parallel, at a global scale, of the enclosure of the land at home - and the common experience of cultural dislocation and despair with native peoples abroad was voiced in England by 'Romantic' artists, poets and architects from the early Nineteenth Century onwards.

The Industrial system has engendered a pollution of the world at the very largest and smallest scales, to the point where the deadliest contamination is often no longer apparent to human perception; yet the symptoms can be read in a dis-eased architecture of monolithic banality or moribund decay. More wholistic ways of building have survived only at the margins.

Green Man, Lincoln.

"Those who speak with understanding must hold fast to the common in all things"

Herakleitos

"Who can England know
Who only England knows ?"

Anon.

Christopher Alexander writes that "in the biological world there is always an immense complexity; and this complexity comes about as a result of a process of minute adaptation, which painstakingly, slowly ensures that every part is properly adapted to its conditions".[1] Annie Dillard suggests that "the basic quality of life to become intricate is both nature's ultimate safeguard against extinction and the source of our delight in it".[2] Through this process of development and the synergy of inter-relationships, things at once become themselves and achieve a transcendant dimension; in places we call this 'Common Ground' "genius loci", in perception the 'saturated complex' and in people, the process of inviduation.

Carving on Norman font, Portchester.

Architecture strives to reproduce this junction of the worlds of dream and reality, or being and form, through a fluid interplay between imagination and materials in the building process. This is the sense of Mies' "God is in the details" or Kahn's "The joint is the beginning of ornament" and his understanding, that the flash of inspiration at the meeting of thought and feeling is a new kind of consciousness. Henry Corbin calls it the "meeting place of the two seas".[3]

"Blind spirit approaches truth
By the intercession of the material
And seeing the light
Is resuscitated from its former submersion"

Abbé Suger 1140

Prentice Pillar, Roslyn.

Auguste Rodin was able to write of Chartres' "scenes that unroll one from the other like the fantasies of a very clear and very delicate dream".[4] The Great Cathedrals reproduce the

archetypal space of the clearing in the trees of the Wildwood
(both the first Common grazing and the first shrine); wilderness
and sacred space, equally, building towards this transcendant
'dimension between'.

Titus Burckhardt writes : "The world is like a fabric made up of
a warp and a weft. The threads of the warp, normally horizontal,
symbolise such causal relations as are rationally controllable and

Prior Byrd's Chantry, Bath Abbey.

quantatively definable; the vertical threads of the warp
correspond to... the qualitative essences of things. The science
and art of the modern period are developed in the horizontal
plane of the material weft; the science and art of the Middle
Ages on the other hand are related to the transcendant warp".[5]

Edward Hyams understood that "while men retain close
contact with the material of which they are made they seem to
acquire a kind of knowledge, a feeling for the pattern of the

whole...".[6] It was not that medieval society was oblivious to nature, rather, like Paul Cezanne, "nature is on the inside... I am immersed in it. After all the world is all around me, not in front of me". Ruskin observed how the imagery of Gothic ornament expresses the whole cycle of the seasons, like some great living organism; from the buds and shoots of stiff-leaf in the springtime of the late Twelfth and early Thirteenth Centuries, the flowers and full foliage of High Gothic from the late Thirteenth Century until the Black Death, to the falling leaves of 'Flamboyant' and skeletal Perpendicular before the winter of the Renaissance. "To the Gothic Workman the living foliage became a subject of intense affection";[7] the Green Man, half human, half plant, was a spirit of inspiration. It was not that the great cathedrals grew out of the ancient forests, rather they grew towards them : "a gradual and continual discovery of a beauty in natural forms which could be more and more perfectly transferred into stone, that influenced at once the heart of the people and the form of the edifice".[8]

Parallel to the enclosure of the land there has been an eviction of the architect-builder from the Common Ground of medieval practice. The Renaissance cult of the individual began with Brunelleschi's breaking of the masons'guild at Santa Maria Della Fiore in Florence and now means, as Berthold Lubetkin put it, that "In the East... each generation stands on the shoulders of the preceding one, while in the West we climb to eminence on the backs of our competitors".[9] As John James points out , a succession of at least nine master masons worked on Chartres Cathedral, yet still produced a unified whole.[10] The separation from the process of building and the inability to make adaptations as a building takes shape, has made architecture increasingly lifeless with each new stage of abstraction : from the pattern-book classicism of the Eighteenth Century and the drawing board schemes and casualised labour of the Nineteenth Century to today's computer aided design and 'cardboard style'. Christopher Alexander claims this is no accident, if coloured pencil drawings and cardboard models are the main media used in design; "the post-modernists have created an almost ludicrous pastiche of cardboard architecture, which vaguely resembles the images of past ages, but without any genuine inner force".[11] "Each change of industrialisation brings economies, but is wasting the world".[12]

If buildings become faceless, so do we - man makes architecture, but architecture also makes man. Sam Webb writes of "the men who have sunk Atlantis : the archiocrats", cogs within cogs of a machine.[13] It is not Utopia which should be on trial,[14] but the system that continually obstructs its realisation. Conversely, Hassan Fathy wrote "when man... is dressing stone he is spiritualising himself and spiritualising the stone".[15]

Both the Victorian battle of the styles - Neo-Classicism looking to an Arcadian Greece, The Gothic Revival to a sanitised Middle Ages - and the Twentieth Century futurist manifestos, are utopian in the sense of being displaced from the present. Kathleen Raine demonstrates how the Nineteenth Century imagination, stifled by the dominant 'logical positivism', took refuge in literature like Lear's Nonsense Verse or Caroll's 'Alice in Wonderland';[16] equally so with architectural eclecticism or today's Disneyfication of cityscape, as a frustrated imagination runs riot. Lubetkin talked about the "startling originality of roaring, snarling, shrieking architecture... a technological fanfare of a shifty age of make-believe,[17] yet Miguel Gonzalez, a Chilean designer, can tell me he has "nothing against British architects except their almost complete lack of imagination".[18]

There has however, been a continual undercurrent, ever since the industrialisation of building - from Pugin, Ruskin and Morris, through the Arts and Crafts and pioneers of the Modern Movement - who understood the neccessity of working collaboratively and with materials in the process of building; part of what Colin Ward has called the 'Moral Left', beating a path to rough ground on the margins of the mainstream. To Aldo Van Eyck, architecture is a kind of outlawry, a sort of contraband to be smuggled in, in spite of all the obstacles.[19] For Henri Ciriani, "being an architect today is like being a monk in the Dark Ages".[20]

"...Our dreams,like the forests buried underneath the highway, never had a chance to grow."

Gill Scott Heron[21]

"The state is the principle of authority - an abstraction masquerading as something real and can have no real contact with the one concrete reality - man himself - whom it treats as though he were just an abstraction".

Giancarlo de Carlo[22]

If the Enclosures movement broke society's relationship to the land, the imbalance created the potential for industrialisation and an emptiness which propelled the British outwards to colonise the world. Edward Hyams writes : "The European conquest of the world for Western Civilisation ... has a superficial air of a dynamic and creative act, but behind which one can detect that fear and despair at the failure of the spirit which accounts for its violent and predatory character... Orthodox historians have consistently failed to perceive that imperialism is a symptom of despair, of deep self distrust in the soul of the imperialist culture".[23] The urban industrial system was engendered by a negation of values, the occlusion rather than the balance of opposites; and seeks always to extend it, seeing only vacant space, perceiving no alternative. The colonial policy of 'divide and rule' or power generation through nuclear fission express this nihilism equally well.

William Blake wrote that the industrial system meant "the enforced idleness of the soul", depending on a deprivation of imagination and familiar surroundings as much as hunger. Just as cloth manufacture was the first to mechanise, peoples traditional clothes were the first to go and then their buildings, becoming entangled in a global market. Ivan Illich writes of working people being physically scrubbed of their aura; (a similar process to the Victorian church 'restorations' William Morris opposed); and the effect of the house one lives in : "tell me where you live and I'll tell you who you are".[24]

Today the psychic engineering of advertising and political propaganda depends on this 'tabula rasa' - an unquestioning mirror-glass blankness - on which to project the chosen images.

The Media mediate with a vengeance, between perception and reality; and Robert Lifton writes of the "thousand mile stare" of the brainwashed.[25]

Those displaced by enclosures who emigrated to a New World found themselves instruments of colonisation - their hopes of escape from the harshness of the Old Order were at the expense of the 'dream-time' of those already living there - even when, as in the case of New England settlers, they brought the practice of Commons and village Greens with them. 'Population movements'is a euphemism for a clearance process where first people, then forests, the soil's fertility, and minerals below ground become resources to be extracted; whether the slave trade which depleted Africa, the exodus of Scots and Irish to North America or the transportation of convicts to Botany Bay.

In the present, the process continues with the stream of migrants to the twilight world of shanty towns along the fringes of major cities all over the Southern Hemisphere, where humanity and civilisation eclipse each other, or with the

Bogota, Colombia - Cocaine capital of the Americas.Narcotics in the void, where architecture and building, humanity and civilisation eclipse each other.

44 deliberately constructed slums of Black Townships in South
Africa, while the 15% white minority occupies 87% of the land.

Until modern times, settled and nomadic cultures held each
other in check, a complementarity similar to the Common
wilderness areas and enclosures of England, but at a European
and global scale. Nomadic peoples' closeness to their land
comes not through working the soil, but through their
migrations, which follow the rhythmical and narrative qualities of
nature, undifferentiated from it; where they see a richness of
associations, civilisation sees only empty space. "Our story is the
land... it is written in those sacred places. My children will look
after those places, that's the law. Dreaming place... you can't
change it, no matter who you are".[26] Yet "almost all our
monetary expressions - currency, capital, stock, pecuniary,
chattel, sterling [and the 'hide' as a measure of land] ...have their
origins in the pastoral world".[27]

Today the Steppes of Central Asia, from which successive
migrations entered Europe or were repelled, have been
ploughed up to grow cotton and the Plains Indians of North
America confined to reservations. But there is a striking
correspondence between the hopelessness of indigenous
peoples, uprooted from their traditional pattern of life - the Inuit
of Greenland, the Navaho of Arizona or Australian Aborigines
anaesthetising their despair through alcohol and television[28] -
and the typical Nineteenth Century figure of the consumptive,
opium eating poet or artist.

The great blossoming of English Landscape painting and
poetry at the turn of the Eighteenth and Nineteenth Centuries is
contemporary with the Enclosures movement; a kind of
compensation in the national psyche for a disappearing reality.
But as with the eviction from three dimensions into two of
Georgian architecture's planar classicism, the page and the
canvas could only absorb so much, before disintegration set in.
Nevertheles they also stand as a record of "a world of pastoral
beauty that could be ours, if we did but desire it passionately

enough";[29] icons to be carried through the desert on our exodus from the land.

The Enclosure of estates to create picturesque parkland, the revival of classical taste, the enormous profits made from slave trading (£15,000 per voyage was usual) and the market for landscape painting are all part of the same paradigm; in which nature is seen as an an object to be 'improved upon' and admired from a distance. "The best way to ensure Summer in England is to have it framed and glazed in a comfortable room" as Horace Walpole expressed it. Both slaves and pictures were auctioned in the London coffee houses.

John Barrell[30] argues that the expropriated poor came to be treated as objects of fear and benevolence just as the landscape came to be regarded as a spectacle, and that the human figures in Constable's paintings became progresively smaller as their presence became less acceptable to his clientele. For Watercolourists Turner and Cotman[31] (and the poet Wordsworth at Tintern) the monastic ruins (often themselves now features of estate parkland) provided subject matter as much as scenes of

Cornfield, Windmill and Spire.   Samuel Palmer 1826

rural life or the wild, sublime and untamed wastes of the nation's uplands.

The circle around William Blake, particularly Samuel Palmer and Edward Calvert, working in the 1820's and early 1830's[32] as the Enclosures Movement was reaching its height, achieved a peak of visionary intensity, perhaps unrivalled in English Art. Palmer writes of Blake's illustrations to Thornton's edition of Virgil's Eclogues, which inspired them : "Visions of little dells and nooks and corners of Paradise; models of the exquisitest pitch of intense poetry... intense depth, solemnity and vivid brilliancy only coldly and partially describes them. There is in all such a mystic and dreamy glimmer as penetrates and kindles the innermost soul...". Samuel Calvert wrote of his father's work as "a constant realisation of Heaven on Earth and of Heaven and Earth happily blending their essentials",[33] but neither Calvert nor Palmer were able to sustain this quality into middle age.

Blake - Illustration to Virgil's Eclogues

John Clare the 'Peasant Poet' who lived through the the enclosure of his village and wrote:
"Ye Commons left free in the rude rags of nature,
Ye brown heaths beclothed in furze as ye be,
My wild eye in rapture adores every feature,
Ye are dear as this heart in my bosom to me"[34]
was a voice for an enormous body of the inarticulate

dispossessed and ended his days in the Northamptonshire lunatic asylum. Today his native Helpston is practically surrounded by vast fields of wheat and barley and skirted to the East by the main London-Edinburgh railway line; in nearby Peterborough the municipality have lent his name to a multi-storey car park.

The Sheep of His Pasture   Edward Calvert 1828

Pugin was unable to come to terms with his grim vision of 'Contrasts'(1836) between the life of medieval cities and the Poor Law institutions of his own day and by the greatest of ironies, spent the last months of his life in the vast neo-classical mad-house in South London that now houses the Imperial War Museum. Ruskin suffered a breakdown and was addicted to opium in later life, while Morris had a stronger constitution but died aged 62 "of being William Morris". Charles Rennie Mackintosh was driven by the contradictions between the art of building and architectural practise to alcoholism and cancer, while more recently Louis Kahn "was killed by greedy men".[35] The establishment of the Royal Institute of British Architects in 1834 was itself an enclosure - of the practice of Architecture.

(In France of the 1890's, Paul Gauguin travelled first to Brittany and then to Tahiti, but found syphills and suicide as well as a culture to work in. Today the region is used for nuclear testing and 200 patients travel annually to Paris for cancer treatment. Tahitian artist Jad recently had his work surrounded by a cordon of gendarmes when he tried to exhibit it on railings near the Louvre).

Intuition and creativity are tolerated by the industrial system, like 'native customs' in the colonies, so long as they are confined to bottom shelf, private, status, or put in quarantine on a pedestal. The reservation and the gallery or 'artists' colony' are reflections of each other; problems only arise when it is suggested that far from being extraordinary, these faculties exist within us all. Romanticism has been the dominant form in English art and poetry since the early Nineteenth Century; an anti-industrial culture in an industrial society, which exploits the contradictions of this Bohemian detachment, rather as the 'artists' quarter' can become the vanguard of gentrification and new investment opportunities.

Thomas Merton writes "the enemies of the artist's freedom are those who most profit by his seeming to be free";[36] and Eric Gill : "This modern world... can give us an honoured place - it cannot, even if it would, give us an honourable job".[37] The 'noble savage' and the 'picturesque landscape' are both examples of a paradoxical ability to idolise and exploit something at the same time, of a system which depends on a spiritual void yet is continually searching for something of life to appropriate and affirm itself. Under these conditions, culture and nature become at once depleted, scarce resources and highly marketable because of their rarity.

What we do to the rest of the world we also do to ourselves; inner and outer developments inform each other. The same conglomerate that mines uranium in Namibia and wants to open workings on Aboriginal land in Australia - RTZ - pollutes Hull with lead, arsenic and polonium. We export toxic waste to Third World countries (The 3,176,000 tons recorded as being shipped from industrialised countries to the less developed world between 1986 and 1988 is described as 'the tip of the iceberg'[38])

The Capper Pass tin smelting works at Ferriby, operated by Rio Tinto Zinc, 'the mining arm of Her Majesty's Government'(according to the Daily Telegraph), of which the Queen is a major shareholder. The plant manufactures the base metal for coin of the realm, but is to close in October 1991 after a local campaign linking the chimney to cases of childhood leukaemia and brain tumours; the cost of clean up operations is estimated to be at least £30 million.

in the same way that fears about the future are suppressed into the unconscious mind : "The silent scream within;... loss of certainty in the future is the pivotal psychological reality of our time".[39]

As we mined the fertility of the land, the gene pool was treated as expedient. Ruskin wrote that the faces of those he passed on his walk to the British Library grew "daily more corrupt" and the proportion of blind and disabled in Hull's population is striking to the incomer. Today the exploitation has become more insidious, because less visible; the endpoint of stockbreeding and enclosures in the 'Age of Improvement' is genetic engineering and the irradiation of food with by-products of the nuclear industry.

"Disturb the delicate intricacies of the limitless microcosm and frighten the angels... if that is what we desire , it will soon be here for there is a limit even to the limitless... We now split atoms... soon it will be the stars".[40] The U.S.'Star Wars' programme envisages particle beams and H-bomb generated X-rays fired from orbiting 'battle stations'; while cashless payment systems and cordless telephones which log the user's whereabouts offer unlimited possibilities for surveillance and the invasion of privacy.

As the mind has become a function of the machine it created, the body has become an increasingly superfluous object of pleasure : in an economy oiled by the free play of science, capital and libido. If we have become the land of 'banking and bonking' in tabloid parlance, of the service economy and 'personal services', Blake was uncompromising in his criticism of the body-politic : "The whore's cry down muddied street, shall be Old England's winding sheet".

If the Nineteenth Century phenomenon of body-snatching and dissection was symptomatic of a society which was carving up the world, perhaps the sale of London cemeteries or the trade in kidneys and living tissue express a near total invasion of the body by forces of the market; it is alleged that handicapped children from Brazil are being sold for organ transplants in Europe. And just as the vast shopping malls and office atria accross North America and Europe pressage a total artificial environment, the artificial womb - from test tubes at one end to incubators at the other - is steadily eroding what human space remains. As Tadao Ando points out, "the desire to belong and the desire to return to the womb overlap".[41] The architect stands in the belly of his creation; we are all in the belly of the beast.

"The Old Triangle goes jingle-jangle
All along the banks of the Royal Canal"

Irish Traditional[42]

Divorced from reality, from human beings, from its surroundings and from the materials of which it is made, architecture comes to embody a profound sense of unease, becomes diseased. In the Nineteenth Century institution, geometry becomes a tool of the state - the vast labyrinthine prisons developed by the Victorians are as much pure constructs of the mind as Piranesi's 'Carceri d'Imaginazione' or the monumental projects of Ledoux and Boullee; (in the 1970's the Shah of Iran's secret police built their prison on a ring shaped plan, so that screams from the torture chamber would echo endlessly around the corridors). The Workhouses of the 1834 Poor Law were masterminded by Liberal followers of Jeremy Bentham - when Blake wrote of 'Dark Satanic Mills' he was referring equally to the materialism of Utilitarian thought as to its built expression. If the Workhouse dissolved the last remnants of the monastic pattern in older charitable foundations, Bentham's 'Panopticon' replaced God as the traditional focus of space with the gaoler. Along Hull's Hedon Road, the Victorian maternity hospital, prison and cemetery stand in a row - the institutionalisation of displacement, giving control of the masses from cradle to grave - and a violation of the individual spirit.

The Classical language became a mask for imperial power and the colonial process; and even in America, where Classicism had

The old Women's Prison from Clifford's Tower, York Castle - a facade of Ionic sophistication 'used to conceal enormous brutality'.

democratic connotations, they were those of a slave-owning democracy. To some it may have had connotations of free thought independent of medieval theocracy, but it has been used to conceal enormous brutalality. George Hersey describes how Classical ornament derived from rites of animal (and possibly human) sacrifice - a sense of the knife concealed in a basket of flowers[43] - while Ruskin believed the Orders were founded on slavery. "Wherever the workman is utterly enslaved, the parts of the building must of course be absolutely like each other";[44] indeed the 'Golden Age' of Augustus coincided with the ruthless suppression of Spartacus' Slaves' Revolt. Slave caverns in Georgian Bristol and Liverpool are the dark side of the well mannered facades behind which they lie, while the White House was built by Negro slaves and the whole of Washington's monumental centre is surrounded by a black ghetto. Demure, appreciable to the educated eye, 'Classicism' has been as much deduced from the front of the Collisseum (which concealed barbarities of its own) as 'de natura deducta'.[45]

Stephan Szczelkun talks about Class in England in similar terms, as "an enormous area of inhumanity in the collective mind";[46] scars hidden when people become Middle-Class, by adopting an uncomfortable veneer of attitudes and behaviour. From its 'Renaissance' in England, Classicism has been something of a superficial imposition - Inigo Jones was as much a designer of masques as buildings, for a Stuart Court regarded by many as alien and decadent. Burlington's Palladian revival[47] also brought opera to England - the forerunner of today's Arts Establishment, the "opera classes", with 'the Arts' becoming part of a power structure as much as culture. To be sure, the language underwent a sea change after its arrival, but as a backdrop to the entertainments of an elite, the seeds of De Chirico's ghostly 'fascist metaphysical deserts'[48] or film-set consumer post-modernism are already latent.

Terry Farrell's 'redevelopment' of London's Charing Cross Station for instance, is a cardboard box of a building - displacing that other Cardboard City, the homeless sleeping rough in Embankment Place. Today the language of Jones' York House

Rosamund lived "at Woodstock where K.Henry had made for her an house of wonderful working... this house after some was named 'labyrinthus', or 'Dedalus'Worke', which was thought to be an house wrought like unto a knotte in a garden, called a maze."

Stowe : 'Annales of England' 1592

"Society is produced by our wants, and government by our wickedness; the former promotes our happiness positively by uniting our affections, the latter negatively by restraining our vices... Government, like dress, is the badge of lost innocence; the palaces of kings are built on the ruins of the bowers of paradise."

Tom Paine : 'Common Sense'   Philadelphia 1776

Blenheim Palace from Fair Rosamund's Well. The Royal Manor of Woodstock was the first Park to be enclosed in England, given to the Duke of Marlborough by Queen Anne in recognition of his military services to the Crown. Blenheim commemorates a battle which put the imperial ambitions of Britain's rulers firmly on the map; the remains of 'Fair Rosamund's Bower' were demolished to make way for the Palace and 'Capability' Brown's landscaping, though it is said that Vanburgh used an existing alignment with Bladon church spire for the main axis of his Baroque drama. Begun in 1705, it cost in excess of £300,000; a bricklayer's annual wage was £25.

water gate (accross the street) has been inflated into 'air rights buildings' underpinned by piles 120 feet deep, mined by hand. Over the river, remnants of the brave hopes of the Festival of Britain sit naked and vulnerable, the young and rootless shivering in its grey corners - the South Bank Arts Complex may be next in line for a cosmetic cladding. Latest proposals for the Paternoster Square area of the City are the visual equivalent of what Orwell called "the rat-trap faces of bankers and the brassy laughter of stockbrokers".

The same right-wing clique centred on Peterhouse, Cambridge, which initiated the 'Architect Bashing' of recent years, as part of a concerted attack on the Welfare State and the Post-War social concensus has moved on to promoting a 'classical revival'. David Watkin's 'Western Tradition'[49] reduces the achievement of the Middle Ages to a 'Gothic Experiment' (when asked for his opinion of Western Civilisation, Mahatma Gandhi replied that "it would be a good thing").

There is a fragile precision about much of the Classical language that almost wants to break; humanity comes to it in ruins (Soane and Speer equally envisaged their projects as ruined), unlike other traditions where form and material renew each other. It is a part of our inheritance that deserves to be understood; many of the 'greats' of the Twentieth Century - whether Mackintosh or Corbusier - had a solid 'Beaux Arts'[50] training. But to be really alive, architecture will always have to go beyond the Classical framework.

"To those of you subjected to the study of Vignola and the 'three orders of architecture' I would like to present architecture's true image. It is determined by spiritual values derived from a particular state of consciousness, and by technical factors that assure the realisation of an idea".[51]

In the hands of Francis Bacon and the Restoration Royal Society, the masonic traditions of the Middle Ages became a blue-print for the domination of nature. Freemasonry has often been a malign influence since it became 'speculative' and opaque, whether its present links to the Ku Klux Klan in

America and the Italian Mafia through the P2 Lodge or simply a
network of back-scratching which ensures the mediocrity of
building in Southern seaside towns or Industrial cities in the
North of England. In Hull, the masons introduced electricity and
cremation.

Pevsner describes the Fylingdales radomes as "the geometry of
the space age at its most alluring and most frightening".[52] Here
architecture becomes reduced to an attitude of 'Design', where
human concerns are dismissed as 'issues of style'; a frame of

Fylingdales Moor; the 'Radomes' are to be transported to Theme Parks
in Arizona (alongside London Bridge) and California.

artificial reality suspended on only the slightest of umbilica. It gives a view of the planet from the outside, but it is a detachment that makes us outsiders in our own world. This highly engineered non-place utopia can never be more than the preserve of a few, with the majority subsisting in the ruins that lie between it and the ravaged Earth. It could also be a nightmare of boredom - less cities, than floating cemeteries of the stillborn, unable to incarnate.

'Without a vision the people perish', but uninformed by the living, utopia becomes dystopia and dreams, nightmares - from Bacon's 'New Atlantis' to Albert Speer's vision of Berlin as 'Germania', the capital of a 'Thousand Year Reich'. Yet as 'Parkinson's Law'[53] demonstrates, the purpose-built headquarters is often an indicator of entropy and decline in the life of an institution - whether Michelangelo's Saint Peter's or Barry's Houses of Parliament - as much mausoleum as monument. The monumental classicism of Hitler's Germany or Stalin's Russia deals only with the collossal - it has no size, proportion or human scale - and is thus unreal; what was once the city has become the parade ground for a mind numbing spectacle of authority. Leon Krier (who has produced an elegant and apologetic volume on Speer) claims that the planning of Milton Keynes New Town resembles Auschwitz. The point is, rather, that unalloyed, abstract rationalism in all its guises, expresses the vacuam of the soul created by the industrial state or corporate machine.

Bruno Bettelheim writes of the physicians who experimented on living subjects under the Nazi Third Reich : "It was the particular pride of these men in their professional skill and knowledge, without regard for moral implications, which made them so dangerous. Although the concentration camps and crematoria are no longer here, this kind of pride remains with us; it is characteristic of a modern society in which fascination with technical competance has dulled concern for human feelings. Auschwitz is gone, but so long as this attitude persists, we shall not be safe from the cruel indifference at its core".[54]

Aldo Rossi talks enthusiastically of an 'Architecture of Death' in

Norman Foster's new building for Independant Television News has close-circuit security cameras the size of a penny piece set into the walls - who's watching who? Any 'Design as the conquest of space' is also a subjugation of the human spirit.

a moribund culture, and just as the monumental cemetery has become a popular theme in Twentieth Century architecture, it is ironic that often cemeteries maintain the only link with the past in Post-War Germany.

If the 'Rationalism' of Rossi and the Krier brothers represents the rigidity of archetypal forms stripped of physical reality (this was the 'house style' used on Internationale Bau Anstellung projects in West Berlin during the 1980's, described as 'the

58 biggest collection of 1:1 models in the World'), "the nightmare of deconstructivist architecture (which) inhabits the unconscious of pure form rather than the unconscious of the architect"[55] is an even further stage of abstraction. Parallel with the advent of 'artificial intelligence' outside any human sphere of reference and the erosion of the body's immune systems by pollutants and epidemic disease, 'deconstructivism' is quite literally a corpselike decomposition of peeling elements adhering to a skeletal framework.

"They produce a devious architecture, a slippery architecture that slides uncontrollably... toward an uncanny realisation of its own other nature... The architect expresses nothing here. The architect only makes it possible for the tradition to go wrong, to deform itself...What is being dissolved is a set of deeply

Bunhill Fields : 'the dead present within the living' - those buried here include Wiliam Blake, John Bunyan Daniel Defoe and George Fox. It formed part of Moorfields, in all probability the Common Land of the earliest inhabitants of London. It is unconsecrated ground, yet in 1484 Warwickshire chantry priest John Rous suggested it was the enclosers who should be denied a Christian burial - why should they share the ground in death if they would not share it in life?

entrenched cultural assumptions... about order, harmony, stability and unity".[56] Aldo Van Eyck refers simply to "obscene antics with building materials".[57]

Fashionable despair and the infinite repetition of the same element in an architecture which mistakes power for life paraphrase Carl Jung's description of the totalitarian state, as the primal scream of the ego at the expense of the collective unconscious. This 'form devoid of content' is nevertheless continually casting about for things to justify its existence ; as Auden pointed out, with the Swastika, the Nazis "pirated the symbol of the universe" - an expression of the innate spontenaiety of life used to validate an oppressive imposed order. This is no less true of the operation of market forces in contemporary Britain, where Margaret Thatcher has claimed to occupy the 'Common Ground' of British Politics.[58] Just as restyled names and corporate images change perceptions without touching the nature of the institution - from Windscale to 'Sellafield' or Department of Health and Social Security to 'Benefit Agency' - the sheen of glamour and cosmetic surgery offer the hollow promise of consumer capitalism, that you can be different from who you really are.[59]

"Even the 'marginality' of the dispossessed can be appropriated... with the arrival of the new Yuppie Internationalism with corporate post modernism as its aesthetic, we have the perfect expression of a culture which... displays a passivity towards the totalising forces, systems of exploitation, administration and control, and at the same time continually simulates signs of 'individuality' to produce a totally colonised but 'irresponsible' subject - the free individual".[60]

NOTES

1. 'The Style of the Twenty-First Century : an Essay on Technology, Geometry and Style' M.I.T. Press 1987
2. Annie Dillard : 'Pilgrim at Tinker Creek' Cape 1975
3. Henry Corbin : 'Temple and Contemplation' K.P.I. 1986
4. Auguste Rodin : 'Cathedrals of France' Country Life 1965
5. Titus Burckhardt : 'Sacred Art in East and West : Its Principles and Methods' Perennial 1976

6. Edward Hyams : 'Soil and Civilisation' Thames and Hudson 1952

7. John Ruskin : 'The Stones of Venice' Vol.II Ch.7 'On the Nature of Gothic'

8. ibid.

9. In Peter Coe : 'Lubetkin and Tecton : Architecture and Social Commitment' Arts Council 1981

10. John James : 'Chartres : The Masons Who Built a Legend' R.K.P. 1982

11. Alexander op.cit.

12. Julius Posener, speaking at European Architecture Students' Assembly, Berlin 13.8.88.

13. Sam Webb : 'Architecture, Alienation and the Omnipotent Admin Man' Architect's Journal 1973

14. 'Utopia on Trial' was the title of Alice Coleman's book (Shipman 1985) ascribing the social ills of Post-War Housing estates to the ideas of the Modern Movement in architecture.

15. James Steele : 'Hassan Fathy' Academy Editions 1988

16. Kathleen Raine op.cit.

17. Huddersfield Winter School 14.2.86.

18. In conversation - Coventry 18.7.87.

19. E.A.S.A. Berlin 13.8.88.

20. Plymouth Winter School 22.1.87.

21. 'Winter in America' Arista Records 1985

22. In Colin Ward : 'Housing' Freedom Press 1980

23. Hyams op.cit.

24. Ivan Illich : 'H2O and the Waters of Forgetfullness' Marion Boyars 1986

25. Robert J. Lifton : 'Thought Reform and the Psychology of Totalism' Yale 1963

26. Bill Neidjie of the Gagudju people, Australia 1983

27. Bruce Chatwin op.cit.

28. "Television is like cultural nerve gas. You sit and watch it and you feel good, and all the time it is destroying your culture and you don't realise it." Eve Fesl Aboriginal Research Centre Guardian 7.12.87.

29. Robin Tanner in 'South-West Artseen' Spring 1987

30. John Barrell : 'The Dark Side of the Landscape' Cambridge University Press 1980

31. John Constable : 1776 - 1837

J.M.W.Turner : 1775 - 1851

John Sell Cotman : 1782 - 1842

32. Samuel Palmer's visionary period is 1819-32 (when he was 18-31). Edward Calvert's is 1827-31 (when he was 28-32). (Virgil wrote his Pastorals when, under Augustus,the Roman peasants were being driven off the land)

33. Raymond Lister : 'Edward Calvert' Bell 1962

34. In Hoskins and Stamp op.cit.

35. A.Komendant : '18 Years With Architect Louis I.Kahn' 1975 : Kahn died of a heart attack shortly after an office building he had worked on for eight years was transferred to Skidmore, Owings and Merril.

36. Thomas Merton : 'Raids on the Unspeakable' Burns and Oates 1977

37. 'Eric Gill : A Holy Tradition of Working' Ed. Brian Keeble Allen and Unwin 1985

38. Jim Vallette : 'The International Trade in Wastes' Report Greenpeace International 1989

39. Joanna Macey : Schumacher Lecture Bristol 11.10.86.

40. Aldo Van Eyck : Milan Triennale 1968

41. Tadao Ando : 'Breathing Geometry' 9H Gallery 1986

42. The song refers to Mountjoy Prison, Dublin

43. George Hersey : 'The Lost Meaning of Classical Architecture' M.I.T. 1988

44. Ruskin op. cit.

45. Vitruvius : i.e. 'deduced from nature'

46. Hull School of Architecture 6.3.89.

47. Inigo Jones : 1573-1652

Richard Boyle, Lord Burlington : 1694-1753

48. Giancarlo de Carlo

49. David Watkin : 'A History of Western Architecture' 1986

50. The 'Ecole des Beaux Arts' in Paris became a model for the education of architects in the Classical tradition in the Nineteenth and early Twentieth Centuries.

51. 'Corbusier Talks to Students' Orion Press 1943/1961

52. Nikolaus Pevsner : 'Yorkshire : The North Riding'   Penguin 1966
53. C.Northcote Parkinson : 'Parkinson's Law or The Pursuit of Progress' Penguin 1957
54. Bruno Bettelheim : 'Surviving the Holocaust'   Fontana 1986
55. Mark Wigley, Princeton in catalogue to exhibition at Museum of Modern Art, New York July-August 1988 sponsored by Philip Johnson. It included work by Frank Gehry, Rem Koolhas, Zaha Hadid, Peter Eisenman Bernard Tschumi etc.
56. ibid.
57. Royal Gold Medal Address R.I.B.A. 26.6.90.
58. Conservative Party Conference Brighton 14.10.88.
59. 'Glamour' originally referred to a kind of illusory magic.
60. Hannah Vowles and Glyn Banks : 'Art in Ruins' Exhibition, London May-June 1988

Imber, Wiltshire : 'Stolen from the People'; when the village was
evacuated in 1943, families were assured it would only be for the
duration of the War. In 1945, they were 'unable to return' because Scots
Guards had been ordered to make the village uninhabitable. The
blacksmith had already died 'of a broken heart' and the Church was
only saved from being removed to Warminster as a garrison church, by
an appeal to the House of Lords - a reunion service is held annually in
September. The Imber Ranges form part of 92,000 acres of Salisbury
Plain occupied by the Ministry of Defence, making it the largest
landowner in the County; the village is now used for battle training as a
simulation of conditions in Northern Ireland.

If so much of our predicament is rooted in an eclipse and negation in the relation between things, a way forward may lie in the idea of dynamic balance - embodied, for instance, in traditional Celtic metaphysics or the wheel of the Four Elements, or in much of the 'New Science'.

Space and psyche can be seen as the basic material of a living process which we at once inhabit and which inhabits us; apparent in the 'leylines' or 'songlines' of the landscape, in the myths and symbols embodied in cities where there is space both for nature and our own inner nature (and where the flow of water is particularly important) and in the geometry of buildings and the relations between people.

The problem of energies and memory unearthed, disembodied and manipulated is evident in our deepest environmental crises and the process of destruction which began with the enclosure of the Commons - yet an understanding of this dynamic of space and its material expression may equally prove a vital tool for healing the wounds.

Specific to architecture this involves building on the 'Modern' achievement, but with a determination to simplify technology, making space and time for the process in which people and place enrich each other - a space more vital than ever, allowing us to take up the challenges of the future.

If ideas about 'nature', 'landscape' or the 'environment' are expanded to the hypothesis of the planet as a self-regulating organism, maybe it is reasonable to credit it with some level of consciousness or memory : the idea of an 'anima mundi'. As localised 'mythos' - the 'Matter of Britain' or 'Albion' for instance - it concerns the relation between people and a particular part of the Earth - something in which we all participate to the same extent we share the common material of which our bodies are made. It may be manipulated by the entertainment industry or the state for reasons of profit or political control - or evoked by the poets, artists or architects of a culture to bring about an intimacy between people and their surroundings, the making of a common home into which we can project ourselves and in which to see ourselves reflected.

The Commons themselves stand for this intimacy - as a co-operative economy, as a memory of the migrations of the first inhabitants of these islands and the struggles of the People against outside domination, or as breathing places for the land.

Understanding the relation between land and society can give us a closer understanding of the built environment, which is, in turn, an index of that relation. It is a relation that has become polluted and estranged, but one which we can begin to strengthen again in our cities - yet remaining mindful that no change can be lasting until we all have the opportunity to be at home in our country.

Breamore Mizmaze, Hampshire - cut into a chalk hilltop, surrounded by an ancient yew-wood.

"Architecture is three-dimensional philosophy"
Berthold Lubetkin

"Commonness is the spirit of Art"

Louis Kahn

If the dominant industrial system depends on a severed connection, a denial of relationship to the rest of life, it is a transcendant common ground of complementary opposites that links us at once to nature and the collective unconscious mind - such that the two correspond. It is also the sense of wonder that lies at the heart of architecture.

Kahn wrote that "Every law of nature... is a part of you...your intuition is your most exacting sense, your most reliable sense" and that "you cannot design anything without nature helping you";[1] while Yeats described "The self which is common to all... he who has thus passed into the impersonal portion of his own mind perceives that it is not a mind, but all minds".[2]

Carl Jung did not invent his theory of archetypes in a collective

Temple of Ammon, Karnak.

unconscious, but derived it from much older ideas of the 'anima mundi' or 'Divine Intellect'. These "archetypal symbolic themes which form the common ground of the human imagination"[3] have bearing on architecture too, if we can understand that the world is larger than Europe and see neglected aspects of our own tradition in those of other continents.

As much as the meeting of inner and outer forms, 'Common Ground' can describe both the base of perceptions and of matter. In many traditions this 'prima materia' is symbolised by water - after all water covers four-fifths of the Earth's surface -

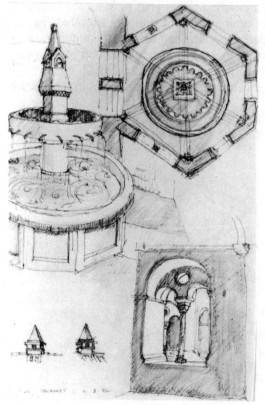

Fountain, Le Thoronet, France.

but it also expresses the flow of space. This is Kahn's 'silence', the primordial darkness of the waters before creation, the 'Yin' of Taoist philosophy and what Illich calls the 'widow of form';[4] the labyrinth or womb matrix, the base of existence, yet transparent and insubstantial.

This is the sense of Richard Jefferies "Sweet is the bitter sea, and the clear green in which the gaze seeks the soul, looking through the glass into itself";[5] and of Le Corbusier's enigmatic statement that "the history of architecture is the history of the struggle for the window".

It is the openings in the walls of a building which very largely give it character, and link the qualitative space inside, encoding the relationship of masses, volumes and proportions which define it, with the outside world. In the same way eyes give expression to a person's face - as "windows of the soul" - it becomes possible to talk of "ensouling buildings"[6] or "living architecture".[7]

Alexander argues that architecture has always been the product of geometry and technology,[8] of form and material combined - an insight that goes back at least as far as the ideas Plato recorded in his 'Timeaus'. In the finished building it is the space itself which forms the Material in this interplay; and in reality neither form nor matter can be perceived independantly of each other. It is only the abstract mentality which sees space as a commodifiable resource to be let by the square metre, a void to be filled, that has thrown the relationship out of balance and spawned a rigid formalism completely lacking in habitable space.

One aspect of our inheritance that has been marginalised that is of interest in this context is the Celtic tradition, which preserves the insights of nomadic people who lived in the Pre-Roman expanses of Northern Europe and were later driven to the upland areas of the West - Cornwall, Wales and the Lake District (Cumbria means 'land of the Cymri') - that form much of the remaining Commons. David Jones writes of "A half aquatic world, it introduces a feeling of transparency and interpenetration of one element with another, of transposition and metamorphosis";[9] while Kathleen Raine describes an "intricate and dazzling web of intermingled elements... more like the glittering veil of 'Maya' conceived by the Indian metaphysics" - "A cosmic sense of the whole implied in every separate part - the past and future in the present, the dead in the living and rebirth in decay".[10]

Celtic Fragments, Saint David's.

Another neglected metaphysical tool is the idea of Four Elements - Earth, Water, Air and Fire , understood as interwoven qualities of matter, acting as vehicles for life and symbolising different levels of existence. In the traditional house for instance,

the 'earth' of walls and 'air' of space form a polarity of shelter
while the 'water' of well outside and 'fire' of hearth inside form
poles around which life is lived.[11] Or in renewable energy
sources the 'earth' of bio-mass or geo-thermal power
accompanies water, wind and the 'fire' of sunlight. Spagyric
medicine based on the balance of these 'elements' in the body
survived well into the Seventeenth Century, while Jung argued
they form a model of the human psyche (earth:sensation,
water:feeling, air:thought, fire:intuition). In this way, the square
of the monastic cloister acts as a symbol of wholeness and well
being; and Le Corbusier's 'Poeme de l'Angle Droite' begins
"dansent la terre et le soleil".

Cloister, Alcobaca, Portugal.

"'The primitive people worshipped springs and forests'. This is said by those who cannot find a way in nature, according to God's precepts; who are deaf and blind in front of the fusion of elements and beings... It remains a mystery what those who recognise the holy places see or hear".

Imre Makowecz[12]

Ivan Ilich[13] describes how the 'waters' and 'airs' of a place absorb impressions of soil and sun, geology and climate, to make a 'sense of place', While Grady Clay[14] argues that a fair ammount of present interest in "genius loci" is a sociological construct of 'spirit sniffers' - "architects, efficiency experts, psychics and hustlers of every kind" - to compensate for the destruction of locality by the multinational economy. Photographs become 'museums of place', as much a symptom of our need to immortalise what we kill, as the landscape watercolours of the last century. The lush foliage of coffee table books and a fad for filters and bottled water proliferate, as local tap water, polluted by nitrate run-off from intensive agriculture, is recycled several times as toilet flush. In a non-place world of computerised inputs, nothing can ever become itself; in 'Silicon Valley', centre of the Californian micro-chip industry, the water table has been deemed too contaminated with heavy metals for agricultural purposes, so it has been designated for drinking. Yet "poking over the horizon, the ancient Japanese art of ecomancy and the Chinese profundities of geomancy have for a long time been sending out early signals to the West. Returning scholars have been bringing back ancient wisdom from these two vast bodies of place awareness... The Chinese discipline of Feng-Shui (is)... a body of rules designed to adapt man's habitat to the mystical forces of the universe'. Its basis lies in the Taoist resonance theory... which holds that the cosmos consists of one interrelated field of energy".[15]

European missionaries in China are said to have been murdered for putting a corrugated iron roof of the wrong pitch on their church and Hans Van der Laan relates the Chinese fable of the king who advised his son to ensure that people sang and

built well, that their hearts and the kingdom should be in
harmony.[16] Johan Huizinga writes of "sacred rites... which...
guarantee the well being of the world... in a spirit of pure
play",[17] like the divine, cosmic game of 'Lila' in the Indian
Upanishads.

There is a remarkable correspondence between these Eastern
traditions (and Western fragments) and much of the 'New
Science'. Things are coming full circle - the new ground is also
very old. Fritjof Capra writes of the 'Tao of Physics',[18] as the
theory of General Relativity has revealed energy and matter as
aspects of the same reality and analysis of ever smaller
subatomic particles shows 'matter' consisting of minute
concentrations of energy in empty space - rather like our own
solar system. James Lovelock formulated the 'Gaia Hypothesis'[19]
of the Earth as a self regulating system, while searching for
criteria to define possible life on Mars. Rupert Shelldrake's
'Morphic Resonance theory of Formative Causation'[20] describes
'chreode paths' created by the repetition of form, which in turn
take on permanence, reality and refinement through this
repetition - similar to the Persian poet Rumi's statement that "the

Cley Hill from Rudge, Wiltshire.

body comes into existence from us, not we from it" (or Kahn's that "man is not nature, but is made by nature") or the way a river makes its path to the sea.

The 'Ley Lines' of the English landscape seem to be part of a geomantic tradition similar to the Chinese 'Feng-Shui', (though much less reputable, because closer to home). Suggested as regulating lines of the Earth's 'subtle body' - lines of energy and water combining to form the landscape - 'Leys' are also intimately connected with a Dreamtime or Mythos, alligning sites with names like 'Arthur's Seat' or 'Robin Hood's Bower'. Sacred places have traditionally been seen as an 'omphalos' or 'navel' linking the physical world to another dimension. Rikki Shields talks of "stories carried in the heart of the people and of the land".[21]

Bruce Chatwin writes of the 'Songlines' of Australia maintained by being sung, where each man's song is like a bird call,at once a territorial statement of his place in the world and a mode of orientation, an oral map - and of poetry and song as the first language. "Yet I felt the Songlines were not neccessarily an Australian phenomenon, but universal : that they were the means by which man marked out his territory, and so organised his social life. All other successive models were variants - or perversions - of this original model... I have a vision of the Songlines stretching accross the continents and ages; that wherever men have trodden they have left a trail of song".[22]

Kathleen Raine describes myth as 'the symbol in transition' - "the highest and most complete form of symbolic imagination".[23] Louis Kahn said the city should be a place where children can see what they want to be when they grow up; equally it should be a place where people can see who they are - "first and last we inhabit a myth : for what is civilisation but the continual creation of an environment of art in which imagination is mirrored... and where it everywhere may discover images of its own internal order".[24] Otherwise, "what yesterday was construction, today becomes nothing but the industrialisation of building... no creation of universal scope can emerge from present culture if there is no understanding or sense of the symbol".[25]

Italo Calvino tells the story of the masons who were too busy to discuss the plan of their city by day, but when night fell pointed to the stars;[26] while Joseph Rykwert describes the cruciform plan on which ancient cities in Europe (and the world over) were laid out[27] : at once the solar wheel-cross and the astronomical sign for Earth, or the circle squared, symbolic of the meeting of Heaven and Earth.

There is a quality of space in these old cities which seems to encourage chance meetings, rather as Herman Hertzberger talks of "formal elements which allow people to be free".[28] With time, the framework becomes overgrown with all sorts of irregular open spaces, courts, back alleys and interesting views, as paths of the feet and eye (or body and soul) interweave with great subtlety, binding the city together and bringing it to life.

Karlovy Bridge, Prague.

There is also space for the flow of rivers and water channels. Illich writes that "the aliveness of a city depends on the bond between a city's water and its flow of dreams"[29] - it is an added dimension to the townscape (and the key to the magic of cities like Venice or Bruges). 'There are only two realities - the mountains and the sea' according to a Japanese proverb; tradition, sometimes likened to a stream, is often strongest in the mountains where springs rise and beside the sea. At 'Block 6' in West Berlin, Eckhart Hahn (who studied in China) recently took the infamous Berlin court and transformed it into a self-balancing micro-climate suffused with light and greenery. Where Engels could write in 1887 that "Berlin has been suffocating in its own maloderous filth for thirty years now",[30] Hahn has used a series of settling tanks, pools and reed beds that clean all foul and storm water from surrounding appartment buildings, allowing it to be recycled as 'grey water' for toilets. Water in the 'moat' around the reed beds is clean enough for children to play in and any excess replenishes the water table, in contrast to the urban desertification caused by mains drainage. Only when the ground reaches saturation does it overflow into the city's sewer system.

Beyond the timeless fields of the Commons, Arcadia or the Paradise archetype, the City is the supreme human artefact - Augustine's 'Civitas Dei', Blake's 'Jerusalem' or Yeats' 'Byzantium'

Cosmati Pavement, Hilandari, Mount Athos.

- where time and timelessness fuse. But as Lewis Mumford pointed out, "we have a great deal of moral repair to do before we shall have cities worth living in".[31] In addition to making space for nature to breathe, this might begin by allowing a return to the unsophisticated spontenaiety of people building their own places to live - because otherwise "people will finally destroy what they cannot build".[32] Rather as the Workhouse, by wrenching people out of their familiar surroundings, severed the connection between 'society' and the individual dwelling, so the designed institution gradually demolished the 'gestalt' of medieval townscape - yet without this soil, architecture becomes banality imposed on blankness.

According to Titus Burckhardt "it is impossible to be engaged in architecture without becoming implicitly involved with cosmology";[33] that is, with the way we see ourselves and the world we inhabit. Olivier Marc[34] describes how in disparate cultures the basic and archetypal geometries of square (body), triangle (soul) and circle (spirit) symbolise levels of human experience, expressed in built form. (It is interesting to speculate that functionalism and its dogma of the flat roof describe a denial of the higher faculties expressed in the gable and the vault; at Ronchamp Corbusier broke out).

Geometry, as Rodin wrote "speaks to our hearts, because it is the general principle of things",[35] the way things take form in nature; just as it is proportion, the relation of parts to a whole, which gives it human scale. Cosmologies, geometries and systems of proportion are many and diverse (just as symbols are many-facetted) - the Chinese, for instance, count five 'elements' (substituting wood and metal for earth) not four. But as approximate interpretations of (or projections onto) the same reality, they usually overlap to a considerable degree - whether, say, the proportional relationships in buildings based around the Golden Section (1:1.618), the Fibonacci Series (1,2,3,5,8,13,21,34 etc), square roots generated by the diagonals of a polygon (1:2 square, 1:3 triangle, 5+1:2 pentagon) or simply a trained eye and developed intuition.

A distinction can be made between mathematical (additive) and geometrical systems of proportion - a polarity of static and dynamic models - the Classical language of the Orders uses the exact fractions and repose of the former, while Gothic derives its innate dynamism from the incommensurables of the latter; (the discovery that mathematics and geometry form different but analogous levels was a crucial point in Greek civilisation - "let no man ignorant of geometry enter here" was inscribed over the door of Plato's Academy). Today we need to integrate both - diagonal based geometries give spaces the inner force of their metabolism; the strings, as much as the sounding-box, are neccessary for a 'frozen music' of spatial echoes. Yet Rasmussen

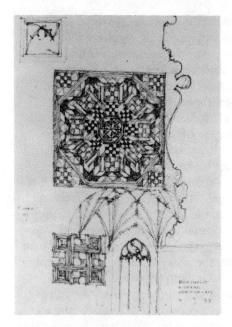

Inlaid Door, Bierthalm.

points out that beyond the proportional geometries of mathematical systems, there are also basic sets of dimensions in building that have to do with human use - that bricks relate to the size of a hand or furniture to the activities of the body.[36]

Just as energy builds up towards the centre of geometric Eastern Mandala structures, Alexander writes of a "feeling of geometrical order and wholeness... in which objects seem centred in space"[37] and spaces centred in themselves, where people can feel at ease and be focussed in their relationships with others. Tom Markus[38] talks of buildings which positively foster a sense of solidarity and conviviality, where common areas are not rigidly controlled, nor private spaces over-compartmentalised, with 'shallow' plans where organisation is innate rather than manifested in barriers and controls. There needs to be a dynamism between path and place, between the containment and free flow of space.

Organisational networks of people - of "insight and compassion" at each intersection of a "jewelled net",[39] "ironic points of light... wherever the just exchange their messages"[40] - and the meridians and pressure points of the body (the lines along which Chinese medicine operates), run parallel to alignments in the landscape and the 'regulating lines' of architecture. Imhotep, architect of the Great Pyramid was also a physician, deified in the Greek Pantheon as Aesclepeos, god of healing; A sense of wonder comes about with the alignment of something we see and something within ourselves.

Sheldon Manor, Wiltshire.

"Our nostalgia... is as much for permanence of ourselves as for
the land"

Keith Critchlow[41]

"Evolution through mechanisation is in some respects a disaster
for the human species... it changes the type of man too rapidly
for him ever to become one."

Antoine de Saint Éxupéry

Nothing material is harmful in itself, rather it is a question of
balance. Appreciating the subtlety of the world we inhabit can
act as a brake on senseless destruction, but introspection in the
face of increasing social repression will not be enough on its
own. To move forward we have to go beyond the game of
"European ping-pong",[42] of grey, no-win binary logic to an
understanding of broader wholes.

Loss of self in the Cosmos is no solution to the destruction of
identity by the State. Dicing with the sublime energies at the
heart of nature and the fascination of totalitarian power reflect
and negate each other; or as Orwell cynically commented
"Emancipation is complete : Freud and Macchiavelli have
reached the outer suburbs".

Indeed the energies of traditional sacred sites (or the
imbalance between land and society) seem to exercise a
powerful psychic pull on the more demonic aspects of
technocracy - in a state of the nation where plutonium has
replaced the gold standard and willingness to 'press the button'
is the new test of allegiance. The Sellafield plutonium works and
Fylingdales early warning station are both in the vicinity of
prehistoric stone circles; while at Hinckley Point nuclear power
plant, which contains a Bronze Age barrow within its perimeter
fence, the authorities keep a plastic pixie as a totem to ward off
accidents. Controversy surrounds proposals for a £15.5 million
Anglo-U.S. radar missile tracking station near St David's - "a
shrine to Welsh Celtic and Christian tradition"[43] and Nuclear
Electric are sponsoring Bristol Cathedral Choir, while the
network of nuclear blast-proof microwave transmitters for
emergency government use are often associated with older

allignments. First Aboriginal sacred land in Australia and now
Red Indian land in the Nevada Desert have been the testing
ground for the British nuclear weapons programme.

There is a touch of the surreal about Norman Foster's
collaboration with a Feng-Shui man on the Hong Kong Shanghai

Royal Observer Corps nuclear fall-out monitoring bunker, Rollright
Stones, Oxfordshire, June 1990; Practice for the End of the World? A
bizarre ritual involving half a dozen grey-suited R.O.C. men, two fire
crews and an ambulance. The officer in charge was keen to stress there
was nothing nuclear about the exercise, they were simply rescuing a
dummy, the annual fire drill. A furniture salesman in everyday life;
"where's Utopia?" he asked, "sooner or later you've got to stop throwing
tomatoes and join society". Looking into his eyes, all you could see was
the back of his head. Echoes of human sacrifice.

Bank project (even to the point of auspicious arrangements of furniture in the drawing office), while the Arch-priest of Hi-Tech himself has chosen to live close to Avebury and the ancient Wiltshire Downs.

"The old Lakota was wise, he knew that man's heart away from nature becomes hard; he knew that lack of respect for growing, living things soon led to lack of respect for humans too".

Luther Standing Bear[44]

'Unearthed', there is a strange and disturbing quality about these energies to the town dweller; just as geometry, uninformed by material, becomes deterministic. Louis Kahn wrote that "if you destroyed the village, you would be destroying the link between nature and a place to live";[45] the Nazi State exploited an overreaction to the destruction of that link, tapping a vein in peasant culture which though respecting bonds of place and kinship had often been inimical to civilisation. Pioneer members of the Soil Association were connected with the British Fascist movement in the 1930's ("the tragedy of our time is not so much the malice of the wicked, as the helpless futility of the best intentions of the good"[46]); it is in the nature of totalism that it contaminates almost everything it touches.

Nature can equally be brutal; Ruskin may have praised 'Savageness' as part of the essence of architecture in Northern Europe, but there is no purpose or virtue in a return to the 'black laws of pagandom';[47] Engels wrote of delivering "the rural population from the isolation and stupor in which it has vegetated almost unchanged for thousands of years".[48] The Peasantry is the place we have come from; it may also be the seed of where we are going, if there is to be space to belong and relate and be fully human. Yet there is a long distance between the subsistence economy of villagers tied to the land and the position today, where what is 'natural' must be a conscious choice in the face of seductive global forces.

We are only beginning to understand (or regain an understanding) that space and psyche, energy and matter, form a continuum - and that when we heal the division between them there is an intimacy between man and nature that allows higher, spiritual potentials to come into play. To those who work the land this understanding of the spirit latent within material is obvious; knowledge that brings with it a simple humanity ('to plough is to pray' as an old English proverb puts it). Electoral franchise can become a surrogate for this intimacy; there is much hypocrisy about 'Human Rights' of freedom of political expression, when access to the land and the right to produce food and construct a dwelling (and to do these things co-operatively) are denied to the majority in the industrialised world. However, this is not yet the experience of most of our fellow human beings in the 'Developing Countries' - 800 million Chinese peasants, for instance, will not be easily shifted. Behind calls for liberal democracy is often a desire for Western consumer goods and a life of ease which too often turns out to be a Faustian bargain.

Democratic institutions are central to the culture of cities, but just as cities without space for nature are unlivable, democracy without popular control is meaningless; as the ideology of the 'Pax Americana' - the 'New World Order' - it verges on the totalitarian. "The liberal democratic revolution and the capitalist revolution are related to one another... there is a very tight relationship between liberal democracy and advanced industrialisation, with the former following the latter inexorably".[49] Orwell had few illusions : "'democracy' ie capitalism, (meant) back to the dole queues and the Rolls Royce cars".[50]

Once projected into the political arena, myths can too easily become lies - Europe has suffered enough from the politics of 'Blood and Soil' - but identity is not the property of a race or nation state. The Green political constituency in England may be roughly similar to nationalist parties in Scotland and Wales, but the point about the 'Green Movement' is that it is more about starting from where you are, than hustings promises that cannot be kept. Beyond shadowing the planetary exploitation of the Multinationals, as Socialism fought the exploitation of people by the first wave of Capitalism, or being tolerated as a comfortable counter-culture, it is about balance and intervention in our present reality. It is not a case of being against progress or growth, but these may be qualitative and cyclical as well as linear, (or, neccessarily advocating a return to wilderness for its own sake). We can only go forward, but so much depends on the spirit in which a thing is done - whether path is a matter of pilgrimage or of tourism, or place concerned with dwelling or possession. There have always been divisions of opinion among those opposed to the dominant order, as to the relative merits or demerits of machinery - political or physical - but if we are ever to make technology a tool, it will depend on our ability to anchor ourselves in a closer relation to nature.

A certain ammount of 'New Age' re-tribalisation is little more than gift-wrapped quarry chippings of the collective psyche, regarded by the advertising industry as the flower of consumer culture; yet rather than ourselves becoming victims of cultural imperialism or any other 'fix' exploiting the spiritual void, the challenge is to see the insights our own tradition needs to recover its sense of purpose and well being, reflected in those of others. The existence of energy networks is something to be acknowledged - a dragon to be tamed and fixed - as a matrix of inspiration rather than any sort of manipulative framework; and it is in the balance of social organisation and natural forces that architecture comes into being, fostering at once an intimacy and a detachment from nature. John Betjaman wrote that "Architecture can only be made alive again by a new order and a new Christendom... It is unlikely that this will be capitalism",[51] yet it is possible to re-integrate something of the body of wisdom (and faith) that underlay the Medieval achievement without waiting for a complete change in economic conditions - perhaps transforming them in the process. The present convergence of the old metaphysics and 'New Science' offers an opportunity to break out of the cycle of nihilism.

Eric Gill wrote of four 'causes' in the making of things - Formal, Material, Efficient (process) and Final (purpose) - in architecture all these elements need to be balanced, otherwise one predominates at the expense of the others. In the present 'pluralism' we see the formalism of Rationalism and Post-Modernism (the 'Rats, Posts and other Pests'[52]), the concern of 'Romantic Pragmatists' for materials at the expense of an ability to tackle large urban projects; the 'Hi-Tech' of Foster, Rogers and Co. which can degenerate into bowellist technological obsessions and 'Community Architecture' which although well intentioned can become a rather thin, Dickensian gruel.

'Battles of the styles' may help media circulation figures, but they also serve to obscure debate about the relationship of buildings to their users and their surroundings; at worst ammounting to 'keeping people in a cage and asking what colour they would like the bars painted'. As Louis Kahn put it "aesthetics come after you make something, not before" and "the false dialectic between traditional and modern architecture is being transcended by pressing environmental concerns";[53] "Tradition is like an arrow pointing to the future... transmission - tradition's real meaning, its reality".[54]

The great contributions of the Modern Movement were its

Spa Green, Finsbury - Lubetkin and Tecton 1946 "I believe in the future and that we build it together;" "We fought the mandarins and won, and we'll win again,because in the end, truth always wins".

understanding of architecture as a social programme - "at stake here is brotherly concern for all - (it) is not a stage set"[55] - and its understanding of the flow of space, of a building as a journey through states of being. Yet with the 'International Style' "ideals crystallised into a stylistic exercise"[56] and an architecture of flux merely emphasised the dissolution of cities already occurring under pressure from motor traffic. Jeff Nuttall wrote that "movement, like drugs, is good tactics but a poor alternative to established culture. It is the temporary denial of existence and existence must be our ultimate province";[57] "Not everyone can have a car, but everyone could have a traditional house".[58]

A building exists - has its being - through its expression in the materials of a place. Market forces and legislation have striven to hold each other in check - as building components and 'archibusiness' come increasingly to reflect the slush of petro-dollars from New York to Tokyo via London - yet neither can generate or foster a sense of place. "The laws of the market require only that buildings be profitable to someone... in this transaction neither the user nor the passer by have any place except by accident";[59] often, 'good architecture is good businesss' only when beauty is in the eye of the shareholder. Before the Industrial Revolution people made the places where they lived; and out of this process architecture grew.

David Lea writes : "An architecture which expresses a

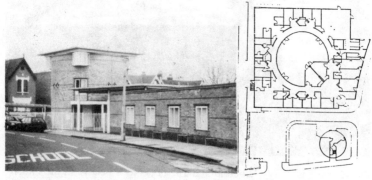

Whittington Day Care Centre, Streatham. Edward Cullinan, Robin Nicholson and Mungo Smith 1984.

planetrary vision, rather than an abstract technological
romanticism, would be, as in the Middle Ages, rooted in its own
region. Though it is impossible to achieve with any degree of
purity these days, we can work towards it if we look for the
non-technological solution at the planning stage, use low energy
materials, include the material's life in assessments of building
costs, start from traditional techniques, simplify and purify
construction details; plan to trap heat and sunlight and avoid
using mechanical systems; cut down hours of alienating paper
work, and help building users take back control of the building
process and the planning and design of their villages and
neighbourhoods.

I think this healing should start where industry first began to
terrorise nature, here in these islands".[60]

"The architect has no other way to endorse his independence
than by driving one wedge after another into the circumstances
in which he finds himself".

Tadao Ando

"We recognise that we are living through the disintegration of a
whole social system which threatens to survive its own death by
entombing us for decades in its own lifeless structures... The
forward march of capitalism continues by way of a 'return to the
past' to consume even the dead, the ruins left in the wake of its
'emancipation'".[61]

It is estimated that most privately owned Commons will have
disappeared by the middle of the next century unless they are
protected by a right of access;[62] and even the 'privatisation' of
National Nature Reserves has been mooted. The Forestry
Commission has been forced to sell 350,000 acres and
privatisation of the water industry has sent a further half million
acres into private ownership (pressure from the Ramblers'
Association managed to secure continued access to only 90,000
acres in the Elan Valley and around Thirlmere and Haweswater
in the Lakes) - as the atmosphere of the country grows daily
more repressive. We are over-loaded with the political and
chemical dross of one and a half centuries of industrial

production, while the world subsists on the brink of ecological catastrophe; the air and water are Commons as much as the land. "The scandal lies not in the system's inadequacies but in its very existence".[63]

Wrenched from land and from culture, humanity is losing its innocence : we are being forced to grow up, as a species, and understand that "we are not only the eyes of the planet, but its communicating consciusness, a planetary nervous system which is useless without a healthy body... while we are in bodily form we are the earth".[64] "The scientific world has ceased to be scientific, notions like subject-object, inner-outer world or body-soul no longer fit"[65] - they are aspects of the same reality. The laboratory mentality has become unsustainable - "we can no longer speak of nature as such. In physics we are no longer investigating nature but nature subject to our scrutiny".[66]

We perceive through proportional contrasts betwen complementary opposites and are confounded by an 'enigma of vast multiplicity' - "our pitiful inability to come to terms with greater number and behave with sanity towards the environment".[67] Our continent is still traumatised by the Second World War and sedated by consumerism and ideology, yet is groping towards a new consciousness. Architecture can play a mediating role in sharpening our perception, providing "a structurally comprehensive refuge to protect (man's) individuality and to calm his spirit";[68] space to deal with the scale of the problem and for a reverence for life and the land. Understanding that the individual is not powerless but part of a greater whole, and that beauty is merely "the complexion of health",[69] a quality that arises when things are true to themselves.

"Common Ground" embodies at once the 'limits to power' expressed in ancient rights to the land and the 'power of limits' - the innate pattern structures of life around which things take shape. Marginalised and yet continually present beneath the surface, as Jung, using the motto of the Delphic Oracle, described the collective unconscious mind - "Vocatus atque non vocatus, deus aderit" : 'invoked or not, the God will be present'.[70]

When things are centred they become 'earthed' into this level; a

vertical, gravitational pull to resist the outward, horizontal force
of the state, the machine or the market.

There is no contradiction between 'social' or 'deep' ecology or
in Orwell's plea for a marriage of intellect and patriotism. John
Berger writes "it would be mistaken to believe that the question
can be reduced to a purely ecological one - important as this is.
It is not only nature which is threatened, but also the survival of
politics and culture - which is to say the survival of human self
respect";[71] he describes the great interpersonal solidarity of the
North as a 'green heart', like a resilient sprout in the present
Winter of the nation. Green lies at the heart of the spectrum. It is
at once 'the colour of nature's bloodstream' and of Robin Hood
and the Levellers; contemplation and resistance feed each other.

Hull is where a revolution began when Charles I was turned
away at Beverley Gate in 1642; it is where Robinson Crusoe
sailed away to find his imaginary desert island and where
Wilberforce and the abolitionists set out to bring an end to
slavery. Today, although the Old Town has lost its ring of water,
its arteries choked with 'festival shopping', the tide still ebbs and
flows up the river; while beyond lie the plain of Holderness and
the 'German Ocean' - a sense of the vastness of the field on
which the echoes play.

The Dissolutions and enclosures have happened; what has
disappeared cannot easily be wished back. The challenge is
rather to reclaim the Commons with "something to give each
separate personality sunshine and a flower in its own existence
now";[72] to make place for those parts of human experience we
call 'Heaven' and 'Earth', and their meeting in the present
moment.

NOTES

1. Alexandra Tyng : 'Beginnings : Louis I.Kahn's Philosophy of Architecture' 1975
2. W.B.Yeats : 'A Vision' Macmillan 1937
3. Kathleen Raine : 'Defending Ancient Springs' 1985
4. Ivan Illich op. cit.
5. Richard Jefferies : 'The Story of My Heart' 1883
6. Chris Day : Hull School of Architecture 29.4.88.
7. Imre Makowecz : 1986-7 Notebooks, not yet published in English.
8. Christopher Alexander op.cit.
9. Kathleen Raine op.cit.

10. ibid.
11. Eg. Peter Blundell-Jones' description of Philip Webb's 'Red House' : Architect's Journal 15.1.86.
12. Imre Makowecz op.cit.
13. Ivan Illich op.cit.
14. Grady Clay : 'Sense and Nonsense of Place' in 'Right Before Your Eyes' A.P.A. Planners Press
15. Ibid.
16. Richard Padovan : 'Hans Van der Laan' 1982
17. Huizinga : 'Homo Ludens' 1938
18. Fritjof Capra : 'The Tao of Physics' Fontana 1983
19. James Lovelock : 'Gaia : A New Look at Life on Earth' Oxford University Press 1982
20. Rupert Shelldrake : 'A New Science of Life : Hypothesis of Formative Causation' Paladin 1985
21. Rikki Shields : Hull 19.6.88.
22. Bruce Chatwin op.cit.
23. Kathleen Raine op.cit.
24. Ibid.
25. Olivier Marc : 'Psychology of the House' 1977
26. Italo Calvino : 'La Citta Invisibile' 1974
27. Joseph Rykwert : 'The Idea of a Town' Faber 1976
28. Speaking at The Architectural Association, London   Autumn 1987
29. Ivan Illich op.cit.
30. Friedrich Engels : 'The Housing Question' 1887
31. In Lionel Esher op.cit.
32. Nicholas Habraken in Jan Wampler : 'All Their Own' Oxford 1977
33. Titus Burckhardt op.cit.
34. Olivier Marc op.cit.
35. In Painton Cowen : 'Rose Windows' Thames and Hudson
36. Steen Eiler Rasmussen : 'Experiencing Architecture' M.I.T. 1962
37. Christopher Alexander : 'An Approach to Wholeness' Architectural Review February 1986
38. Tom Markus : Hull School of Architecture 21.4.88.
39. Joanna Macey op.cit.
40. W.H.Auden : 'September 1, 1939'
41. Keith Critchlow op.cit.
42. Aldo Van Eyck : Berlin 13.8.88.
43. Reported 14.4.90.
44. Chief Luther Standing Bear : 'Land of the Spotted Eagle' 1933
45. 'What Will Be Has Always Been : The Words of Louis I.Kahn' Rizzoli 1986
46. Thomas Merton op.cit.
47. Saint Patrick : 'The Deer's Cry'
48. Friedrich Engels op.cit.
49. Francis Fukuyama, 'adviser to the U.S. State Department and the Rand Corporation', Guardian 7.9.90.
50. George Orwell op.cit.
51. John Betjaman : 'Ghastly Good Taste' 1933
52. Aldo Van Eyck : R.I.B.A. March 1981
53. Pierre D'Avoine : 'Reality and Project : Four British Architects' exhibition at 9H Gallery July 1990
54. Corbusier op.cit.
55. Ibid.
56. Berthold Lubetkin : Bristol Winter School 1983
57. Jeff Nuttal : 'Bomb Culture' Paladin 1970
58. Abdelwahed El Wakil : U.I.A.Congress   Brighton 1987
59. Andrew Saint : 'The Image of The Architect' Yale 1983
60. David Lea : 'One Earth : William Morris' Vision' in 'William Morris Today' I.C.A. 1984
61. Hannah Vowles and Glyn Banks op.cit.
62. Marion Shoard : 'This Land Is Our Land' Paladin 1987
63. Rudolf Bahro : 'The Logic of Deliverence' Lecture   Bristol 11.10.86.

64. Keith Critchlow op.cit.
65. Nils Bohr quoted by Aldo Van Eyck : R.I.B.A. March 1981
66. Werner Heisenberg ibid.
67. Aldo Van Eyck : Milan Triennale 1968
68. Hassan Fathy op.cit.
69. William Lethaby : 'Architecture : The Modern Position' Oxford 1955
70. Carl Jung : 'Memories, Dreams, Reflections' Collins 1983
71. John Berger : New Statesman 11.3.88.
72. Richard Jefferies op.cit.

Rose Window, Beauvais.